WOMEN CAN DO EVERYTHING

YOU ARE THE STRATEGIST OF YOUR LIFE

Written By

Patricia Szriftgiser

www.PatriciaHealth.com

Skinny Brown Dog Media
www.SkinnyBrownDogMedia.com

Published by Skinny Brown Dog Media
Atlanta–USA and Punta del Este–UY
www.skinnybrowndogmedia.com
Distributed by Skinny Brown Dog Media
Translation Services: Skinny Brown Dog Media
English Developmental Editing and Design by Eric G. Reid
English Content Editing by Timothy Swiney

Spanish Edition Published by PanHouse Casa Editorial
www.editorialpanhouse.com
CEO: Jonathan Somoza
Production Manager Paola Morales

Publisher's Cataloging-in-Publication Data

Print Book ISBN: 978-1-957506-19-7
Ebook ISBN: 978-1-957506-20-3
Spanish ISBN 978-980-437-081-6

Women Can Do Everything may be purchased in bulk for educational, business, and fundraising purposes. For information, please email:
Patricia.Szriftgiser@gmail.com

WHAT OTHERS ARE SAYING

"Patricia has so much knowledge of human relationships and psychology that her ability to show you alternative paths and guide you to see new possibilities for solving critical situations is unmatched. It is incredible the transformation that one can create in one's life if they simply listen to her and follow her prompting.
Marisa Lisa, New York -USA

Patricia Szriftgiser's professionalism and excellence as a psychologist and life coach has elevated and taken my life to a higher level than I could have ever imagined. It is an absolute pleasure to be her client for so many years, and I will continue with her forever.
Silvina Pianzolas, New Jersey - USA

If anyone has a unique perspective for any problem that comes their way, it is Patricia. She has always had a creative and totally different and innovative angle to make you think and reflect, solve and create positive changes in life. She is highly effective in her interventions and proposed solutions.
Daniel Diaz, Buenos Aires- Argentina

When I hired Patricia Szriftgiser, I did not know that our relationship would be so fruitful and so long. I have worked with Patricia for years at every stage of my life. Wither I needed a touch of therapy or just to gain insight from her wisdom. Without a doubt, she changed my life, over and over again. I can say that I am grateful for her and everything that she did in my life because it changed my life.
Liliana Groisman, Tel Aviv- Israel

Doc Patricia (that's what I call her), my guru, listens attentively and respectfully and validates what you feel and then suddenly she gives you feedback so accurate and so profound that you have no choice but to take action and elevate yourself. The strength she transmits to you is immeasurable and makes you want to experience your best life.

Paulina Ramrez, Naples-Florida USA

DEDICATION

To my parents, Santiago and Susana Szriftgiser, your legacy is my life example. It is my north, my compass, it is strength, intelligence, ethics, adaptability, integrity and deep respect and love for human *beings and life*.

ACKNOWLEDGMENTS

Thank you,

To my parents, my family, my brother Gabriel, you are the "figurehead" of life.

To Barry, my husband, a man who is unconditional in everything he does and gives.

To my admired and adored friends in my life: Adriana, Claudia and Monica.

To my new and found good friends.

To my patients, to my ancestors, to my past self.

To all the women who inspire me every day, I am eternally grateful for all of you.

All paths are valid, but you should always remember a path is only a path, and if you think you should not follow it, you should not, under any pretext. Your decision to stay on a path, even when it seems wrong, must be free of fear and ambition. And to have that clarity of mind, you must lead a disciplined life. Only then will you know any path is only a path, and you will not be afraid to leave any path when your heart tells you.

Watch each path carefully and deliberately. Then ask yourself this question. It is a question that only old people ask. My teacher taught it to me when I was very young, and my blood was too vigorous for me to understand it. Now I understand it. The question is:

Does that road have a heart?

If it has, the way is good; if not, it is useless.

There are some roads that have a heart and some that don't. Some give you a pleasant journey and you become one with them, others leave you lost along the journey. Some make you strong, the others weaken you.

The problem is that no one asks the question; Does that road have a heart? And when man finally realizes that he has followed a heartless path, and the path is about to devour him, few are able to stop and deliberate and abandon it.

For me, the only thing worthwhile is to travel roads with heart. On them I travel, and the only challenge is to cross them in their entire length.

For them I travel and travel observing, breathless...

Your existence will be made with all the threads of the loom, like the lives of all men. That you will not lack, nor will you have too much, a single opportunity to make of your life what you want it to be. And if you will be one thing and not the other, it will be because, in spite of everything, you will have to choose?

May the force be with you.

The teachings of
Don Juan Carlos Castaneda

CONTENTS

FOREWORD

A book is a reflection of the author. It is a piece of both who they are and their work. It is intended to extend the values, principles, morals, knowledge, and purposes to which they have invested many hours of their life into. Far more hours spent than required to write a book with the hope of communicating an idea or belief.

This commitment and passion is why it is an honor and also a pleasure to tell you about Patricia Szriftgiser. Patricia has poured her wisdom and experience into these pages.

Patricia is an example of a woman whose life and profession are dedicated to the service to others.

Besides her high level of professional excellence and vast knowledge, she has established herself as an internationally recognized mental health care professional with a career that spans over twenty years of work around the world. She has been called upon to provide care for front line workers and their families in some of the most horrific of situations.

Patricia is someone that maximizes every moment of the day in her professional and personal life. She is always learning and developing new techniques in her clinical practice and as a life coach all with the single goal of serving her clients at the highest level. She also has an impressive ability to find and create solutions that benefit those who have been guided by her.

I might add that she is an unwavering agent of change and strategic planning, never leaving a detail uncovered, working side by side with her patients and clients to ensure that the process is enjoyable, deep and intense, in order to achieve the desired goal.

It is easy for me to talk about Patricia because I have known her for over twenty years. She is someone in my life I deeply respect for a myriad of reason. A further testament to her level of professionalism is that she was chosen by my friend Rivka, who offered to be her mentor. Few people were lucky enough to be chosen by Rivka, an internationally recognized mental health expert and speaker, author in her own right.

Doubts of her ability to achieve results do not exist when you see the result of her work with patients. Anything Patricia agrees to be a part of becomes high caliber. Her professional standards always ensure a final product of the highest quality.

Women Can Do Everything is good because she combines all her knowledge and experiences to create a book that is both useful and personal, aimed at promoting physical, intellectual and emotional growth.

Something extremely important in *Women Can Do Everything* is her ability to share real-life cases that readers will easily identify with and learn from.

Within the pages of this book, you will find the clarity to better connect with yourself and with others and transform your life.

Patricia proves that success is not exclusive, and that everyone deserves it and can achieve it.

Dr. Michael Meir
Psychotherapist
TEDX Speaker Consultant - Trainer and Educator
(Coaching in Human Development)

PREFACE

This book was born in my mind and in my heart. I have been working for over forty years as a professional in the mental health field: twenty years in Argentina and twenty years in the United States. It has been a very fascinating career. My professional practice is attending to the diversity of cultures of so many powerful and beautiful women.

From those experiences and the knowledge I gained, I want to speak to the heart and soul of women who feel dejected, confused, or need guidance on this journey we call life. In this book, you will find testimonials taken from my consultations with women just like you, describing various issues that together we have dealt with over the years of clinical practice. You will also find a few strategies and ideas on how you can transform your life. This book is written with sincerity and love, in the hopes it will help you find your way again. I have called this process the "departure without horizon" because, inevitably, we will find ourselves in a place of uncertainty of the road ahead and facing new realities. In this book, I offer you guidance on how to start that journey into the unknown.

This book is for all women who reach a certain age and perhaps feel that they have lost a certain splendor. As I read somewhere: a woman is a princess at fifteen, beautiful at twenty-five, passionate at thirty-five, unforgettable at forty-five, a lady at sixty, special at seventy and beautiful all her life. I share this to remind you that each stage has its charm and that a woman is always beautiful, regardless of the circumstances she finds herself in. There is, and always will be, beauty beyond the physical appearance.

As I write this, I am sixty-two years old. From my experience as a psychologist and a high performance competitive athlete, I have a lot to offer to that woman of fifty-five who does not know what will happen to her at sixty; also, to that woman of twenty-five who fears what she will face in her forties.

In this book, you will find a path that starts from where you are and leads to an uncertain horizon. Along the way, you will begin by recognizing your feelings and learn to validate and understand each of those emotions.

We will also discuss grief and its link too many of the circumstances we encounter and also to recognize that this word is not always related to the physical death of a loved one. I will tell you stories of patients who have traveled these roads, so that you discover that no matter how isolated you feel, you are not unique or alone. Despite the circumstances, there is always a path, a way out, and I will help you to travel it.

To walk along this path, we must first accept that we are on it by going through a process of acceptance and recognizing our own identity.

After recognizing yourselves, you will also go through a stage of learning to value yourselves and rediscover that feeling of loving yourselves. In doing so, you will discover the wisdom of what you are truly capable of doing and rebuild yourselves.

Don't worry, we will take this new adventure together. Together we will chart a fresh course. You will not be alone. From this moment on, you will have a traveling companion who will provide you with the tools so that your journey will be smooth and solid. Together we will find that new horizon!

I put in your hands all my experience as a professional and as a woman. I offer you my knowledge to help you answer each of the questions that may be overwhelming you in the face of new realities.

This book is an authorized translation of *Women Can Do Everything: Eres La Estratega De Tu Vida* written by Patricia Szriftgiser, originally published in Spanish in February 2022 by Editorial PanHouse.

The translation team at Skinny Brown Dog Media has worked closely with the author to preserve her voice and teachings, while making her wisdom available to the English audience.

Enjoy!

"When we can no longer change a situation,
we have a challenge to change ourselves."

Viktor Frankl

CHAPTER 1

MOVING INTO THE UNKNOWN

Recognize You?

There comes a time in our lives as women when we look back and see the road we have traveled and think of all the untraveled paths along the way. We can choose to look at our past with regret and remorse or decide it is time to take ownership of the road yet untraveled. The road ahead is always unknown, and moving forward can be filled with fear and doubt. But it can also be filled with excitement and anticipation.

I want to share the stories of women not so unlike you that have stood where you now stand. And allow their stories to help you prepare to move into the unknown that awaits you.

Maria is a woman and a mother who had dreams and wanted to do many things, but because of her commitment to being a good wife and a dedicated mother, she set her personal goals aside. Her time to reflect came when her children were grown and no longer needed maternal support. She had dedicated her life to providing them. All the plans and decisions she made focused on either her role as a mother or as a wife. Then suddenly, she realized that she was no longer the central driving focus in the lives of her family. She could no longer give orders to her children, as they now had families of their own to manage. Faced with this unknown future, questions arose in Maria's life. Questions like; What do I do now? Where do I go next? What do I do with the rest of my life? What role is next for me?

Maria had attached so much of her self to the role of wife and mother that she had lost a clear sense of her identity when those roles shifted. For Maria to move forward, she needed to be willing to accept that a new role awaited her. One that she was free to create and recreate as she chose.

Let me share a bit with you about Ana, a woman who was not a mother but was an aunt, a sister, and a friend. Ana had a successful career. She had chosen to put her carrier before marriage and everything else. Then one day, standing in front of the mirror, she realized she had neglected her physical health in her pursuit of a successful career. Somewhere along the way, the fitness and natural advantages of her twenties had slipped away. Ana did not regret the success she had achieved, but a part of her longed for the Ana of her youth, full of energy and engaged in outdoor adventure.

Ana's moment of reflection was not so much about regret but awareness that in committing herself completely to her career, she had lost focus on other equally important parts of her life, mainly her health. Her unknown journey ahead would be discovering how to maintain a balance between career and health. And about exploring what it would feel like to release a little control at work to regain her overall well-being.

Francis's story is not unique. She, like many women, got married thinking it would be for life. Only to find out that was not to be her reality. Years of unhappiness passed, and there came a time when she recognized that the marriage she had dreamed of was not the story she was living. Infidelity led to disappointment and the realization that the marriage needed to end and the need to find a new path forward in her life. She found the courage to finalize her decisions. However, the road out of the marriage was filled with challenges and intense emotions. When the day came that her new reality was one of being on her own, she was invaded by doubts and fears about the uncertain road ahead.

Francis's fears and doubts following the end of a marriage are not uncommon. She had invested her trust and faith in another person. She had built her dream of happily-ever-after with someone who later betrayed that trust and shattered that dream. The unknown road ahead would require her to rebuild her ability to trust, dream, and live independently. Francis had to navigate the road ahead with a weakened sense of trust in others and her ability to make sound judgments.

Clara loved her role as a mother and being in a relatively full marriage. Her marriage had its difficulties but, for the most part, was "good." However, almost to her surprise, there came the point when she found herself attracted to a female friend. This level of attraction was something she had never experienced before, leading her to question her sexual orientation. Clara knew she had to discuss her feelings with her husband, family, and four children. It was only after these conversions that she decided to end the marriage.

For Clara, the road ahead required great courage to end the marriage and pursue unknown love. Clara's level of courage did not come without a cost, but she moved forward, knowing that not doing so would leave the unknown unexplored. Today, Clara and her partner Lexie live and love each day together because of Clara's courage.

As a mental health specialist, I can tell you that moving forward following the death of a child can be one of the most complex and challenging decisions. So, suggesting Rosa, a mother who lost her son suddenly and tragically, to find a new path forward was not a simple task. I could empathize with her desire to remain in grief, but I also knew that she needed to move past the grief and into the healing that could only happen by choosing what her life would look like in the future and taking action to achieve it.

After forty years as a mental health professional, I could share many stories of women who each reached a point in life that required them to reflect on the past and determine an unknown path into the future. The stories I shared may not be a direct parallel to your story. But like all women, you will reach a moment in your life that will require you to look back and prepare to move into the unknown. The truth is, you will reach this moment several times in your life. In each of those moments, remember you have come a long way, and that along the journey you accumulated a lot of experiences. You have grown professionally and personally. Your relationships have changed, and as a result, you are not the same woman you were twenty years ago.

You will also reach a point when you look ahead towards the unknown horizon with many of the same questions, I hear other women ask: "What now?" "Where do I go?" "What do I do now with this life?" "What will I do with my time?"

All these women I introduced you to and so many more are going through or have gone through an endless number of emotions and asked the same life questions you may be facing.

The most important thing to remember when you reach such a point in your life is to recognize your feelings. Stopping and taking the time to validate your emotions is one of the most critical steps to moving forward. As a mental health counselor, I have seen many women trapped in rage, anger, frustration, hopelessness, and sadness. A critical question I ask my clients during a session is: "what emotions does your experience invoke in you?" So many times, because of the complexity of emotions they are experiencing, they cannot label what they are feeling. For that reason, I invite them to sit down and reflect on their situation and pinpoint and validate each of their feelings. By separating each emotion and labeling it, they start to understand why they are feeling what they are feeling and become honest with themselves. It is critical to be honest with yourself. Learning to be comfortable with your feelings and feeling those feelings sincerely can make you feel depressed and angry. However, whatever you are feeling and however profoundly you feel, it does not take away from the fact that you are a healthy, beautiful woman.

Recognizing your emotions is the first step in moving towards the unknown future. Perhaps you are unsure where your next journey will take you. Guess what? None of us know about our next journey in life. The important thing is to start walking in the direction you feel called toward. When I reflect on forty years of professional experience and the hundreds of women I have helped, recognizing their emotions and making the right decisions was more manageable because a specialist supported them. This is not to say it can't be done without a specialist. After all, women are strong, courageous, risk-taking, capable, and part of a network of other powerful women. You may not know those other powerful women's names yet, but they exist. They have existed for generations. They are the women who have gone before you, who now wait to be asked to come alongside you. By recognizing your emotions, acknowledging our situation, and moving into the unknown, you find your sisterhood of supporters. Don't underestimate your abilities. Most of the time, if you take a little time alone, you can recalculate, rethink, reassess a new possibility and carve out a new destiny for yourself.

I want to give you a few options to find that new path. To offer you the guidance to move forward when faced with any circumstance or change. You can trust what I share because I am not speaking as your best friend, sister, aunt, or mother. I am speaking as a person with over forty years experience guiding others forward. I will always be the person who will give you the complete picture and show you the many paths you can take, because there is an answer to each of those common questions. "What now?" "Where do I go?" "What do I do now with this life?" "What will I do with my time?" All these questions have answers.

There is always a way forward, and you will find it, I guarantee!

If you look closely, you will see that in each of the stories I shared, there was one common feeling—the feeling of grief.

What is Grief?

Grief is not a feeling associated only with death. Sigmund Freud (1856-1939), a neurologist and creator of the theory of psychoanalysis, wrote countless articles, essays, and books on grief and mourning. In *Mourning and Melancholia* (1915), Freud defines grief as: "A reaction to the loss of a loved one, of an equivalent abstraction as the homeland, freedom, an ideal, among others." Interestingly, this author not only refers to grief as a consequence of having lost something tangible, but also relates it to the loss of ideals or ideas that one presupposes. Freud said that we could experience grief without it being specifically associated with the death or loss of someone.

Going through loss or grief will trigger emotional and behavioral responses. The process of mourning or grief starts with recognizing the lack or absence of something, accepting the loss initially, and not denying it. There is no defined path for grieving. Each person processes grief in their way, and in their own time. The degree of intensity is proportional to the perceived magnitude of the loss or the meaning the person associates with the loss.

Grief may begin before the actual loss itself. For example, there are many relationships in which grief appears before the relationship's final breakup. The anticipated grief can occur consciously or unconsciously or when a person has a terminal illness. The idea of death begins to be dealt with before it happens, before the actual physical death or loss.

However, to overcome the grief process, it is necessary to experience the absence. Freud would say that once the libido has been withdrawn from the lost object, it (the libido) can be directed to attach to a new object. Grief is not a disease but a normal conscious and unconscious process. It involves accepting the loss and giving up all hope of recovery from what was lost. To see and start a new path forward consists of going through various stages that are often easier with the help of a specialist.

In the above work, Freud tells us that life itself, given its dynamics, comprises a set of losses. For Freud, the word "loss" is synonymous with castration. This path of grief, loss, and acceptance can occur at any point. Therefore, conscious and unconscious ability to manage death and grief will generally be more developed at some stages than others.

Freud explains that the individual has developed the bond with an object over time. The object has been given life or the qualities of a living object on which one's narcissism is projected totally or almost totally; so much that the person has been left empty of libido, and it is the object that absorbs nearly all of it. Consequently, when this object is lost, i.e., love, work, homeland, and other significant objects, the person loses their libido or drive and mourns its loss. It is for this reason that Freud identifies in his explanation of grief the presence of significant deviations from normal behavior: sadness, loneliness, disinterest in the external world - the person is only interested in that part of the external world that refers to the object—Freud also points out two inhibitions:

- Inhibition of the capacity to work (create, produce).

- Inhibition of the capacity to love. So, grief is sadness and pain and creates inhibitions of the self.

Grief occupies the subject's life. There is no interest in other things. The person can spend the day only thinking about the lost object. This is where Freud says that the work of grief brings into play the subject's relationship with reality.

Accordingly, it is necessary to find the right path forward, identify reality, and consider replanning. The absence, the emptiness, or the loss must lead at some point to the acceptance and the search for new goals.

Stories of Others on this Journey

I want to share a story about grief and the acceptance of the reality of the loss and the path forward.

I would like to share Liliana's story. She is a 58-year-old woman. Her life was complicated, her father was an alcoholic and abusive, and her mother was submissive, passive, and afraid. In the home she grew up in, there was domestic violence daily. Liliana had two sisters and three brothers, six children in all. She was the middle sister, a circumstance that complicated her life from an early age. Several things led her to become dependent on drugs and attempt suicide more than once during adolescence.

Despite a very complicated life and the circumstances under which she grew up, as an adult she achieved significant accomplishments. She married and had a daughter. Life would have been perfect, except her husband was complicated. The man she married ended up being a replica of her abusive father, and her life as his wife was a reality that mirrored her mother's. Somehow unknown to her, she had recreated her parents' marriage in her marriage. A few years into their marriage, her husband began using drugs and having money troubles, among other problems. The situation led her to decide, inevitably, to divorce him to protect her young daughter from what she feared would be a repeat of her own experience as the daughter of an alcoholic, abusive father.

Following the divorce, she got a job, fell in love, and married again. A few years after the divorce, her ex-husband committed suicide, leaving her with her six-year-old daughter and with the commitment to support her psychologically in the face of this emotional situation. Undeterred, she prepared herself academically to improve herself and get a better, stable job. Her power has been to know how to emerge in challenging situations.

In consultation, Liliana expressed her desire to divorce her second husband. She said that there was no more love in the relationship. With fears and apprehensions about this new unknown reality she would be moving towards, we began to plan together. First, we compiled a list of her talents, values, possibilities, and what she could do. Next, we identified her goals and objectives. During this process, Liliana expressed how she always wanted to be a role model for her now twenty-two year old daughter, and show her she could be happy and move forward in the face of adversity. As Freud said, life is inevitably related to loss at some point. Liliana sold her house, rented an apartment for a year, and prepared for living independently. Despite the circumstances she lived through, she decided to start over at 58 years of age and succeeded. I spoke with her recently, and she has moved out of the apartment and bought the house of her dreams in the city where she always longed to live. She feels complete and happy. Her new path is now being designed by her beliefs based on the work of knowing, identifying her feeling, knowing her resources, and moving into action.

Fear is often the byproduct of uncertainty as one faces a new path forward during times of change.

As I said before, a woman who can identify her feelings and has the strength to recognize them and self-reflect will make better decisions and become happy and loyal to herself. With the guidance of a specialist or support team, the outcome of those decisions will always be better.

I know you may be overwhelmed by doubt in the face of so many realities. You may find yourself constantly asking yourself: "Will I be able to do it?" "How do I design it?" "How can I find a new direction?"

As I have told hundreds of women before you, I am here to tell you that you can achieve whatever you want. Trust what I am saying for now, and later, I will offer you the tools to move forward confidently and with determination to reach new goals.

"What you deny subdues you,
what you accept transforms you."

Carl Gustav Jung

CHAPTER 2

FINDING ACCEPTANCE

What is Acceptance?

I invite you to reflect on what the meaning of acceptance is. How do you develop a level of acceptance in your life? Before we move forward, let's focus on understanding the bigger meaning of the word acceptance. The word acceptance has its origin in the Latin word acceptatio, which means *the action or process of being received as adequate, typically to be admitted into a group.* We can add to our understanding through the contributions of Francisco Franco in his article *Acceptance: Guiding our emotional well-being.* In this article, Franco shows that acceptance is the capacity to assume life as it is or to accept reality, pleasant or unpleasant, as the situation is at face value. Acceptance is a process of tolerance and adaptation, but not of struggle. From the position of acceptance, you can overcome complicated life situations and advance in your personal growth.

To choose to engage in the process of acceptance, you take control of your past and current emotions. Choosing acceptance does not mean the waters will be calm. On the contrary, within the process of acceptance it will be required that you take the helm firmly, assume a positive disposition with joy, faith, and hope, and chart a clear and safe course forward.

It is essential to emphasize that acceptance is a necessary process that you must go through if you are to reach your full potential. And let me also point out that acceptance happens in stages, or phases, and can take time. Therefore, each step of the acceptance process deserves to be recognized and fully worked. Only then can you experience and feel that sense of empowerment and security in your decisions that come from receiving things as they are.

My forty years of experience as a mental health professional allows me to share with you the four stages of acceptance, not only from an academic perspective but also from the perspective of someone who has assisted hundreds of clients to go through the process.

The First Stage: Start

You can only identify the need for acceptance when you realize that something is persistently not right, and you are repeatedly presented with the need for change. To gain the need for acceptance, you must make paying attention to yourself the priority. For example, when looking at a particular situation, you may feel stagnant, confused, sad, and have doubts and uncertainties, indicating a necessity to evaluate and reconsider the situation. During this process of self-evaluation and introspection, you must be willing to ask yourself how you are feeling and be honest with your answers.

Once you can identify the emotions you are feeling and the need for change, you have taken the first step.

The Second Stage: Development

This is the stage of *doing the work*. It must be developed conscientiously, and it requires dedication and introspection. This may be the most challenging stage because it calls into account the character of each woman. *Doing the work* means not putting it off, despite the desire to do so. *Doing the work* requires moving forward regardless of how much fear, uncertainty, or doubt we may experience. Yes, you need to feel confident that doing what needs to be done will result in something better than the current situation.

To begin moving into action, start by asking yourself these questions; "How do I feel about this situation?" "How much is it affecting me?" "Why does it affect me?" "How is this situation different from the experiences inside my comfort zone?" "What should I be learning from this experience?" "What can I control, and what can

I not control in this situation?"

These questions are about putting your awareness into the present moment. By being aware of your reality and accepting it, you can take better actions to change the situation. Before moving forward in a new direction, you need to have a clear perspective of what is happening and what has happened. So often, I see women trying to move forward without fully and honestly answering those critical questions. Without clarity, it will be hard to understand that the changes we need to make will somehow improve the situation. Remember that acceptance is not a straightforward task, but when we accept the situation freely and without personal judgment, we can decide to move forward.

Acceptance allows you to see yourself with love, appreciation, and the absence of grudges, reproach, or negative emotions. Remember, you are taking control of your destiny. Many of my clients have a hard time with guilt-free acceptance. Don't worry. It will happen. Just keep asking yourself which things about this situation do I have control over? The answer will lead to you understanding yourself, and your next actions. The next step will allow you to move forward, grow, and take on the risk of change.

The Third Stage: Ascending

Ascending is the beginning of the third stage of acceptance and the creation of the new you. Stage three gives you the closure necessary to start a new beginning and ascend from the old situation. Ascending is the foundation that will launch you into a solid future. Not taking the time in the second stage to complete the acceptance process would be like building a house on shifting sand.

If you have accepted your current situation and have done the work as required in stage two, GREAT! Now it is time to move forward and ask yourself those big and most important questions: "What now?" "What do I do with all these feelings I have?" "What decision should I make next?" "And perhaps most importantly, what will make me happy?"

It is important to emphasize that all three stages of the acceptance process are yours alone. Seeking the answers from within is an act of loyalty to yourself. It is your life, and you get to decide which direction you head next. It does not belong to anyone else. You must put your interest and well-being beyond any circumstances. It is your ability to ask the hard questions and find the tough answers that are most important on this journey of change.

You must embrace the reality that you are living out a process. Sometimes, when we look at our situations and the past, guilt can take over. Let the guilt go. It does not serve you in this process and you don't want to build a future out of guilt. At the time, you did what you knew to do. Now, you have a different awareness, and you are making different choices. So again, let go of the guilt. You can't have guilt and acceptance at the same time. Acceptance allows releasing the guilt while taking ownership of the situation. After all, the situations are in the past, and even if you wanted to change them, you can't. Take control of what you can and release what you can't; the past is something you can't control. During stage three, you are ascending to a new level of thinking and behaving, and to do that you must remain firm in your convictions and positive in your abilities to succeed.

The Fourth Stage: Closing

Stage four requires that we put a little pressure on ourselves, and that's fine; I even recommend it. That little extra pressure and self-accountability will help us push ourselves forward and get out of stagnation and that old unhealthy situation. The actions required in stage four are about setting deadlines, limits, and concrete objectives as part of an actual plan for change. Procrastination is counterproductive right now. Doing nothing is doing something. It is entering into an agreement not to change, so do something every day to move forward with your plan. No matter how small that action looks, it is one step further away from the old you and one step closer to the new you.

Time passes for all of us, and when our decisions are based on a sense of acceptance, those decisions will put us on the right path. Trust yourself. You can do this and so much more than you can see right now. The sooner we make these decisions and take action, the sooner our reality will shift, and we will ascend to a new level of living.

My Personal Experience

At some point in time, we have all gone through situations that required us *to do the work;* I am no exception.

I was thirty-eight years old. I was living in Buenos Aires, Argentina. A friend of mine suggested that I meet a friend of his who was visiting from New York. My friend said we had a lot in common and would hit it off. I flatly refused by offering a series of reasons. My parents lived nearby, and I was a professional with a successful career. I had my lifelong friends, hobbies, and competitive running in Palermo. Honestly, I did not need to move to another country, let alone meet a man from New York. My life was calm and comfortable, and I saw no need to leave my comfort zone. I was doing what I wanted and how I wanted, all on my terms.

This friend's suggestion of a meeting with this gentleman by pointing out our similarities and shared interests was not enough for me to leave the safety of my comfort zone, not even for a drink or dinner with friends. Oddly, just like me, he refused the suggestion of our mutual friend as well. His excuse was the great geographical distance between the United States and Argentina. If something came of the meeting, it would be impossible to maintain a relationship over so many miles. Despite our mutual resistance, our friend gave him my email address. Little by little, we wrote to each other. We started getting to know each other and, finally, he came to Buenos Aires for a weekend visit. When we met, the connection was immediate; we fell in love at first sight. You could say we were both pulled out of our comfort zones and into each others' arms.

Over the next two years, we alternated traveling to see each, spending three or four days at a time together. It was "comfortable" at the beginning for both of us to manage our relationship this way. We each wanted to keep our independence and still be together. But when I turned forty, I decided it was time to reevaluate this relationship and my life as a whole more seriously and more in-depth. The reality was that I was undoubtedly in love, and I loved the idea of living with him, even though my parents, my great friends, and my professional career were in Argentina. I wanted both worlds, and circumstances would not allow it, so I had to make a choice. But first, I had to become aware of how I was feeling, take control of what I could control, and finally get uncomfortable long enough to decide to change something about the situation

I had to go through the stages of acceptance I outlined above. I accepted my reality and had to think about what that meant. I might be about to leap into the void and change my lifestyle, culture, language, and customs for an idea I had utterly rejected just two years earlier. If I made this decision, I would be leaving my family and friends behind. To fully commit to what could happen next, I had to do a lot of internal work. I had to become a strong, intelligent woman capable of making these decisions without guilt and self-judgment. And only when I could feel guilt-free about my decision was I able to close the book and stop evaluating, recalculating, replanning, and ascend to the next level of my life. I had to decide and leap. Once I let go of the guilt, it became so much clearer about what would make me happy, and in the end, that is what is most essential.

The good news is that my parents supported me immediately and unconditionally. They kissed me on the forehead and told me to do what made my heart happiest. My parents are wonderful people, genuinely unique and wise. They allowed me to move forward free of the quilt I was carrying about leaving them behind.

While on the topic of parents, I will include a quick reflection: Children have their own lives, and they are not there simply to fulfill the parents' personal needs. When the time comes, allow them to go freely into the world with the tools you have given them. Let them live their own experiences, trusting that they will achieve their goals. Allowing them to move forward guilt free can be a magnificent gift—to both parties.

So that is how my life changed, and I ended up in the United States with the love of my life, whom I almost never met because I was afraid to leave my comfort zone. I arrived as a determined woman, firm in my convictions. Sure, I had to consider all the variables that could come into play. But I knew everything was a process of change, adaptation, and new beginnings in every sense, yet at 40 years old, I jumped in without looking back. I accepted the ending of my old life and embraced my new beginning

As scary as life can be, you must always look forward. Work with conviction, power, and emotional self-regulation to make everything you planned work as imagined.

Just so you know, I did a lot of running those first few months, and it offered me the time to be alone with my thoughts and feelings and remind myself that I was on the right path, even though I did get lost from time to time on the streets of New York. So my advice is if you are a runner, run; and make extra time for yourself as you move forward into the new you.

Things have worked out well. Today I am married to the love of my life. We have amazing children and grandchildren, many friends, and a vast collection of race day t-shirts. The amazing thing is my friend was right, and we are both high-performance and competitive athletes. So, we train together and run races together. It's a lifestyle that fills our life and offers many adventures. In moments of significant change, you find yourself looking forward with the promise of something new, filled with great emotions and expectations to what you are about to live and experience. However, you are keenly aware of what you are leaving behind. In my case, it was my country, my culture, family, friends, professional life, and work stability. Each of the losses I experienced could be considered a micro-grief of what could have been and was not, but in every process of acceptance, some regrets and failures are necessary to experience. Then, we choose either to get stuck in grief or choose acceptance and move forward.

I want you to be fully aware of the process of both grief and acceptance, and that we must take ownership of both. You don't have to do it alone, but you must be willing to put in the work.

I had to make tough decisions, but they were always based on my well-being. Today, I am convinced that the results have been gratifying. In every process of growth and change, there is a moment of transition and possible chaos, but with time, dedication, determination, and patience, everything stabilizes. I have never stopped taking care of my parents. The process of how I care for them has changed, but not the level of love and respect I give to them. I have established myself professionally, and I have also maintained my sporting life. These things continue to fill me with satisfaction, and many new experiences and opportunities have been added because I chose to go through the process of grief and acceptance.

Twenty years have passed since I said yes to my new life. It is clear in my heart that I did what I had to do, which was difficult, but necessary. I invite you to see yourself from my story, that perhaps you are at the moment of needing something different, a new experience, and are unsure of what to do. Maybe my story will give you courage and help you understand that all of us approach change with a level of fear and grief. But what I know and you have seen from my story is if you do the work and make the necessary decisions, complete the process of acceptance, and change what needs to be changed, you will look back knowing in your heart that you did the right thing at the right time.

I would like to supplement what you have just read with the following: almost 30 years ago, I began to study Neurolinguistic Programming (NLP) as part of my professional growth. During one training, I was with my teacher in a one-on-one session. He asked me the following question: "Who is the most important person in your life?" I answered quickly and without hesitation "Well, my parents." He immediately replied, "No, you. YOU are the most important person in your life." That is why, in the process of becoming aware, it is paramount to consider your desires and priorities first. You must be able to make decisions despite external opinions and current situations, and the priorities have to be of personal interest. You cannot set limits on yourself based on other people's views. Everything is possible if you want to achieve it. I reaffirm that this acceptance process has only one owner, YOU!

The Acceptance Methods

Although I previously provided you with a simple technique, I would like to offer additional information so that you can use what comes closest to your needs. Each technique or tool is dependent on the case. Some you can develop naturally and independently; others need professional support. Either way, I offer them as resources you can implement as needed.

A fundamental practice of acceptance is mindfulness. Mindfulness is a technique that includes various fundamental elements, which I will share with you now.

1. **Don't judge yourself**: Evaluate yourself with love. Look at yourself with affection, and do not criticize yourself.

2. **Patience:** Don't look too far down the road; instead, focus on what is right in front of you. Don't get ahead of yourself. Stay in the present.

3. **Have an open mind**: Accept all the emotions you are feeling, then work on them one by one. Initially, it is essential to recognize all the emotions you are experiencing.

4. **Avoid fighting**: Let your emotions flow, even if they are conflicting. Don't deny them and don't antagonize them. Let them flow. As I explained, we will work through these emotions one by one.

5. **Trust:** First, trust in yourself and, second, in the professional who accompanies you.

6. **Accept:** Acceptance is the way to inner peace. When you are aware of the process of acceptance, and when you go through the process step-by-step, you find inner peace.

7. **Go forward:** Going forward occurs the moment you are ready to plan the next step. Let yourself flow,

and stay alert for what is coming.

Review these tips to become more mindful, and if you want to delve deeper or look for similar techniques, you can find a lot about mindfulness on the internet. Then, look for techniques that you can incorporate into your daily practice.

Another tool that I invite you to use is journaling. Take a moment to write all the judgments you have about your life, relationships, and current situation. Let it flow. Dedicate at least five minutes each day to your journaling.

- Write down your ideas, thoughts, and emotions. Do not put up filters, let each idea flow, don't worry about the aesthetic details right now, and let nothing stop the need to express what you feel.

- Be grateful for being here. As I explained before, what you are going through is what had to happen. It is part of the process of acceptance and understanding what you cannot change and what you can. So be grateful for every moment of the journey.

- By being open-minded about everything and for everything, write from a position of truth.

- Do activities that give you time to think like running, walking, dancing, yoga, cycling, or any action that makes you feel you are recovering time for yourself. Use this time to refresh your thoughts.

I have the clearest thoughts when I run. My family knows if I add an extra mile or two or ten, I have a lot on my mind I need to work out, and they just give me the space to do so. As a result, I have the best ideas and a great sense of well-being when I finish. So do what gives you joy and pleasure and creates the space for you to have those inner conversations and encounters with yourself.

The steps I shared are general because we are each unique in our characteristics, weaknesses, and strengths, and there is no specific method in all cases; that is to say there is not a secret formula.

I suggest that when you recognize what worries you, what you question, what calls to you to take a deep look at your life or situation and perhaps make a change, you immerse yourself in that process. Remember, the path is awareness, acceptance, then action. Nothing will change without you and your acceptance. But with change, your mind and heart will open to a world of infinite possibilities.

"Life is a journey, not a destination."

"All adversity and all pain
prepares our soul for vision."

Martin Buber

CHAPTER 3

IDENTITY

What is Identity?

We use the word *identity* almost daily as we talk about identity theft, brand identity, or personal identity. So, what does the word identity really mean and what does it mean on a more personal level? If I were to ask you: what is your identity?—what aspects of yourself, your life, your different roles, would this question bring to mind? Your identity can be formed according to your nationality, family group, political perspectives, religion, or profession. We don't just have one identity, we are a composite of many identities that we take on and off throughout our day in our career and/or life.

In this chapter, I want to help you answer the question, "What is identity?" More importantly, what is your identity and does it fit who you want to become? When we started this life journey we each had a unique identity and over time that unique identity has become lost or maybe overwritten by the identities assigned to us by others.

Based on my experience as a psychologist, I can tell you there have been many studies on identity, specifically on personal identity versus social identity. To start, there is the work of an American psychoanalyst of German origin, Erik Homburger Erikson, who put forward an interesting theory in developmental psychology regarding the development of identity.

Erikson, who often references Torregosa and Sarabia, shows multiple meanings to the concept of identity, linking identity to terms such as personal, ego, and self. Thus, sometimes identity will refer to a conscious feeling of the individual; other times, to an unconscious desire for continuity or personal character; or, sometimes, to the synthesis functions of the ego and, still at other times, to the maintenance of inner solidarity with the ideals of a group. So, identity is complex, but don't give up; I will help you detangle it.

I can tell you that identity is considered a subjective phenomenon of personal elaboration, symbolically constructed in interaction with others. A person's identity can also be linked to a sense of belonging to different socio-cultural groups with which we consider having affinity. Identity is built from birth and added to over time based on our interactions with others. Our identity starts with our first social interactions, mainly with our parents and immediate family. Over time, it expands to include school and continues to grow to include each environment we interact with. In today's world, those interactions can be both physically and virtually. Each interaction creates an impression of how we see ourselves, how others see us, and how we believe others see us.

From birth, we are consistently being influenced, and those influences shape our beliefs. As infants, it starts with the bonding between mother and child. Then, gradually, the child builds their own beliefs and mental schemes or awareness, becoming aware of their existence both separate and connected to their environment. The more environments, the more influence and thus, the more ways our identity is shaped, transformed, and reinforced.

Your identity is not just linked to your environment or your relationships, but to time. I mean, *you* are currently at a different you from any other point in time. You are constantly growing. Personal identity arises as a result of various elements. For example, as we have already mentioned, gender identity, political choice, moral values, religion, personal customs and traditions, aesthetic style, verbal and behavioral expression, hobbies, profession, and studies, among others. This is how the person's relationship with herself and those around her is constructed.

So, in summary, or at least for this book, can we agree that your identity is an accumulation of social interaction, experiences, and a few predetermined factors, such as gender and race. And who we are, or our identity, is how we see ourselves, how others see and impact us, and finally, the way we perceive how others see us and our experiences with others. Moreover, this personal identity continues to grow both consciously and subconsciously until our death.

To illustrate how identity is both a perception of self and perception held by others and not always the same, I want to share the story of Camila. Camila was a girl others often described as impatient. This identity was assigned to her based on an experience of someone else, but she incorporated that identity into her internal perception. You probably have done the same. For example, when describing yourself, you may have said something like, "others say I am impatient." That external perception became part of your internal dialog. When you we asked, "tell me about yourself," you responded by echoing what others had said or how they had identified you. As Camila matured and interacted with other people and had different experiences, she realized that the identity of impatient didn't really reflect her and her nature. Instead, she realized she was genuinely tolerant and was, in fact, a patient person. Her initial internal identity was wrong. When she understood who she was and was able to validate with feedback from friends and peers, she transformed that identity internally and externally over time through relationships and a process of internal acceptance.

John Locke, a seventeenth-century philosopher, states in his research that man is born as a *tabula rasa*, an empty mind, a blank slate. As people are educated, both formally and informally, they are encrypted with ideas, beliefs, and values. They are molded by their life experiences and the information they receive from others as part of those experiences. As a mental health specialist, I am opposed to this psychological theory, which may be a basis for constructing the concept of identity. At birth, I believe we bring elements from our parents, grandparents, great-grandparents, our culture, regardless of origin, migrant Europeans, enslaved people, and survivors of world wars, among others, with us at birth. We carry generational identity energy in our womb that is transmitted to a child at birth. These are elements that make up our identity, and that identity grows through childhood and life experiences and interactions. We are not born as *tabula rasa* or blank minds, but a rather full and complex tapestry of history locked in our minds. This generational identity energy or cellular memory is also known as genetic memory. Our identity is formed from both lived experiences and genetic memory. Identity is both who we are based on our experiences and what we bring into the world from the experience of our ancestors. Identity is always observable and comparable, and you just need to know how to see it.

This inherited memory shows up when I hear stories from my grandmother that it was the norm for a child to take up to nine days to open her eyes. Nowadays, children are stimulated at birth. They are able to turn over in a few weeks, not to mention when they grow up and you give them a cell phone, they are capable of doing complex tasks with no training. Locked within the child was a level of knowledge on a cellular level that was accessed as needed. Every day you sit at your laptop without knowing how it works, you can perform thousands of tasks by accessing the coding contained in the software with a few simple keystrokes. Our brains are hundreds of millions of times smarter and more complex than your laptop. Why would it seem impossible that they have access to a set of software we know nothing about? When it comes to understanding our mind and how it operates, we have not touched the tip of the iceberg

An infant during the gestational period receives a variety of external stimuli simply by default as mom, aside from being pregnant, is managing the home, working, exercising, studying for exams, and engaging with people. Mom is a whole person living a full and whole life rich in experience, and each of those moments is shared with the developing fetus. With the complexity of today's world and the multiple roles women play in society, the gestational experience is no longer the same as it was a generation ago. These complexities directly influence the identity of our children pre- and post-birth. All these interactions and experiences become part of the genetic memory, helping to form the genetic identity. I don't want to share all the data and precepts put forward by Locke because some of the evidence distracts from the theory of gene identity. Nevertheless, they are observable facts that construct the concept of identity and impact our overall identity.

To further the importance of the process of identity construction, we can look at one of the characters presented by the prominent writer Joaquin Salvador Lavado Terjon, an Argentinian cartoonist who goes by the name of Quino. In his cartoon in Mafalda, there is a character named Susanita. Mafalda was a comic strip I read daily as a girl, and I loved the character Susanita. All Susanita ever wanted to do was fulfill her role as a mother. She had no other interest. Everything she did in one way or another was related to that intention. Being a mother was the only role that made sense to her. That was how she identified herself. For those who have read Malalfa, you will recall that her passion-filled conversation was insistent in expressing her unwavering desire to be a mother and have the perfect family. It would have been interesting to ask: what would have happened to Susanita if she did not achieve her ideal of being a devoted mother and wife? Would she, then, find herself in a great conflict of identity?

That question of identity and lost identity is not only for Susanita but for all of us at some point in our lives. The question of what happens when you lose your bearing of what you thought was your identity? How do you move forward? How do you create a new identity?

This idea of lost identity occurs to every woman at some point. As I have previously illustrated, it most often happens at the moment when you feel the need to reevaluate your priorities. That moment when you need to take a step back from your life and ask those critical questions. Those questions often start by looking at what you have done and consider how you feel based on what you have accomplished thus far in life. For example, suppose Susanita had maintained an identity that contained a belief system that her only real value as a person was to become a mother and create a family, and that identity had been the sole guiding principle in her life.

What would happen if Susanita did not achieve that identity? She would be forced to evaluate and redirect not only her life but her identity and personal value. Susanita is not alone as a woman who has had to face the question of "who am I now?".

As a mental health professional who has helped women for over forty years answer the question, "who am I?" I began to wonder why do so many of us have to rethink and course correct our identity in our forties?

Understanding Self-Analysis

As we mature, we may have many identities; daughter, mother, employee, professional, friend, wife. All the roles that we as women fulfill in life seem to be connected to other people and our relationship with them. Yes, they provide a very fulfilling part of our identity, but as those relationships change and become more complex, we lose our identity. Yet, we live within those roles, and from time-to-time crises may occur, and new identities are placed on us and others we assume as our own. For example, in today's multi-generational family structure, many women I have met have become caregivers to their elder in-laws. A role they were never prepared for and yet one they must quickly adopt.

Life is like a river. It is constantly flowing. There are changes in our roles and our adaptations to our identity. In some seasons, the river flows freely; in other seasons of our life we feel like someone or something has placed a boulder in our path. In order to move forward and reestablish a sense of purpose, it is necessary to observe these shifting roles, understand how and why they are shifting, adapt and change them to fit the roles we want to continue, and rethink one's that no longer fulfill us.

I think of how many women thought they had the ideal job, a quiet life, they were living comfortably in their comfort zone even with its ups and downs? Then, the COVID pandemic arrived. No one could have prepared or predicted the impact it would have on our lives, our business, and our mental health. So many people lost their jobs. Companies closed or laid-off workers. Suddenly, we were left without the direction our work provided and were thrust into in social distancing and isolation. Overnight, many women went from being a CEO to the role of home-school mom; from having active full social calendars to binge-watching Ozarks on Netflix. So many rapid identity shifts and losses. The whole world had one common question, "What do I do now?"

During the peak of the pandemic, I assisted many patients in finding their "new" identity in the middle of a rapidly changing world. One of my patients, Claudia, worked as a personal trainer for the past twenty years. She had built her business and personal identity among the many group clients and one-to-one clients she served throughout the week at several local gyms. It was her life, her passion. Helping others achieve fitness and personal health was her purpose.

The pandemic changed everything for her. Gyms closed, one-to-one fitness training was restricted by state-mandated social distancing guidelines. Overnight, her business, her social interactions, and her ability to express her passion vanished. Claudia was a 52-year-old who no longer had the routine she had spent the last twenty years building. She no longer had a way to connect with and support others. She had lost what defined and identified her. And the most challenging part was that she didn't know when, or if, she could start to rebuild what she had lost. She knew things would shift, but to what degree only added to her uncertainty.

This situation led Claudia into severe depression. She felt she had lost the battle to be who she wanted to be, which triggered old beliefs and soon old behavior patterns. She began eating and gaining weight. She simply could not stop the spiral of depression and emotional eating. She could not find a direction to follow. When she sat with me that first time, she clearly needed help to create a new sense of identity and value. To get started, it was necessary to propose an evaluation process. I needed Claudia to become fully aware of her current circumstances, and only then, by knowing where she was, could she better identify where she could go.

As I explained before, we start from a process of radical acceptance of reality. This is accepting what we have and, unfortunately, what we cannot change. Accepting what had happened to her fully and completely without judgment or blame was necessary to move to the next step. Claudia could not just stay in the acceptance process if she wanted a new life. She had to ask herself what other function she could fulfill, what personal strengths she could take advantage of in this new reality, and redefine what she was passionate about?

Finally, after reevaluating her position and rediscovering her passions, she saw new possibilities. Like many, she allied herself to the only resource that the pandemic allowed since its beginnings, technology. She started slowly serving her clients again via Zoom. She managed to adapt what she did best and found new ways of relating to her clients, and in doing so, she recovered her identity and added a new layer to her business and the types of experiences she could provide her clients. This was not an overnight transition, but eventually, Claudia was able to stop the negative behaviors that had only added to her isolation and depression. She had found a path forward and saw the light to guide her. She managed to get back in shape emotionally and physically. She reconnected with the people she used to train and added new clients. Later, as the pandemic restrictions lifted, she was able to return to her work as an in-person personal trainer. The crises not only allowed Claudia to adapt but to reevaluate herself, her purpose, and her passions and bring her identity in alignment with these discoveries.

If we take a moment and look closely at Claudia's situation, we can see things that might give us a few clues about finding our own path forward when faced with unexpected change. The first clue is how she initially reacted to adversity? Followed by other clues, such as what new point did she reach, how did she get through it, and how did she manage to overcome it? These are all excellent questions to ask yourself to reevaluate what we are made of, and learn what you need to know about yourself when you face a new reality. Learning to accept the processes can make a tremendous difference. For example, over the years, I have noticed that those who faced great difficulties, that those who approached things from a victim identity versus survivor identity, have greater difficulty in making the shift and adapting.

The pandemic has helped us understand that circumstances and challenging moments are not eternal. All adversity has a beginning and an end. Circumstances are only obstacles; they last as long as they have to last, and we must be prepared to overcome them and reinvent ourselves. The boulder in the river only slows the river for as long as it takes for the river to find an alternative path to the sea. Therefore, we must seek solutions to adversities, which in itself will be part of our identity process. This acceptance of the situation and moving forward leads us to a new identity: resilient. Resilience is the capacity to be flexible in the face of difficulties or the ability to adapt and see new opportunities and face situations from a perspective of progress and growth.

Do you see yourself reflected in Claudia's situation? Most days, many of us do not feel resilient. What occurred with Claudia is one of the many experiences I have had in coaching women through this new pandemic reality. The idea of helping women understand that resilience has more to with recognizing and valuing our own identity than jumping back in the ring to fight on. Resilience makes us grow as human beings. By loving our strengths and incorporating them into new experiences, we become better individuals. Resilience and growth are a cyclical and constant process of reflective learning and changing.

I would like to share a personal experience within this learning about identity. As I told you, I am of Argentinean origin. My father, a man capable of speaking eleven languages, brought me up in a home where you would hear English, French, German, Hebrew, Yiddish, and Flemish, among other languages. Because of this, I am fascinated by languages. I love to link a person's language or languages to a part of their identity process because it is so much a part of my own. However, when I came to the United States and had to communicate only through English, I had to incorporate this new language in its entirety; all my relationships and interactions became mainly in English, which led me to change my Argentine accent a little and also the speed at which I spoke.

Friends would still be distracted by my wild Spanish-speaking flying hands, but slowly over time, I learned to adapt them into my new language and language culture.

Although I frequently travel to Argentina, it is curious and, at the same time, somewhat frustrating that when I am in my homeland I am asked if I am from Argentina or somewhere else because I have lost the little details that make me appear as a native speaker. Within languages, there is an identity that goes beyond just the words, and when you leave the culture, although you may keep the language skills, you slowly, over time, lose the culture linked to that language. This situation is now part of who I am. I am now an outsider within my community. I had to change my behavior, my speech, and even thinking into another language, which is a somewhat complex mental process. Sometimes I have to read in Spanish and understand English or vice versa. I know my origins, but I have had to change my language identity. Language is a big part of my identity. It seems simple compared to the previous example, but learning to speak a new language full time has led me to adapt to different circumstances. I have had to take advantage of my ancestral gifts and turn them into a strength in all my experiences. Those strengths allow me to listen, understand and help others from different languages without losing my origin or a part of my identity.

Building Positive Anchors

When some of my patients come to my office and feel that they have lost their horizon or their North Star and are showing signs of anxiety, I ask them to take a minute and think back to a moment when they felt extremely happy. Then, I ask them to share what they were doing in that moment of complete happiness, who they were with, and any other details that want to share. For example, in Claudia's case, she said she felt happiest during her morning routine, training herself physically, training others, and going to the gym. When she was able to identify that moment and sit within that moment, she was able to place herself back into that emotional state and that feeling of happiness. Once she had shifted out of anxiety, I could show her she should control her emotional states and, when needed, return to a state of happiness and claim victory over anxiety. By being able to remove herself from the anxieties and uncertainty, she felt she was able to gain control and make better choices. Mental health practitioners call this process ANCHORING, and I invite you to incorporate anchoring and use it in your life, especially when you feel anxious or overwhelmed.

Anchoring is an excellent and powerful tool to reset your emotional energy state and your emotional identity.

I will give you some background about the anchoring technique, so you know its origin and can feel more comfortable using it to help balance your emotions. Anchoring in the psychological field is associated with what we call "conditioned reflex." A conditioned reflex is part of the Russian physiologist Ivan Pavlov's (1849-1936) studies through the experiments he conducted by conditioning a dog's feeding with a specific sound. This reward, stimulant, and response process was then coupled with the development of neurolinguistic programming. The technique was implemented during the 1970s in the United States by Richard Bandler and John Grinder, who established the relationship between neurological processes, language, and behavioral patterns. Understanding these two studies will help you develop the reprogramming skills needed to achieve the objective of moving between negative and positive energy states.

Anchoring is incorporated into the techniques used in NLP. Let me show you how. Start by remembering the aroma of a favorite meal made by your mother. What feelings and emotions are triggered in you as you recall that smell? Can you taste that delicious meal in your mouth? Does thinking about that meal lead you to a feeling of happiness and peace? The anchor, in this case, was a smell that was linked or anchored to an emotional state. Anchors can be a word, a song, or an image that evokes a pleasant emotion or negative emotion and sometimes even a physical sensation. When I work with clients with severe trauma or PTSD, they often have many triggers that evoke negative emotions and physical sensations. Helping them disconnect the triggers and their emotional state is not always easy, but it is possible—often by guiding them to create positive trigger emotional patterns. To develop your anchor, I invite you to perform the following exercise:

- Find a place to be alone and quiet.

- Make yourself comfortable.

- Close your eyes.

- From this moment on, you will imagine you are looking at a movie screen on which you will project your thoughts.

- Imagine this big screen with a uniquely sharp definition.

- Take a moment and project a time where you felt extremely happy. Sit back and relive that movie as it plays on the big screen. Study all the colors, see how clear and vivid the picture of happiness is, and pretend the movie has smell-a-vision. What aromas filled the air? What are the soundtracks that you hear?

- Put that image or happy moment on pause.

- Connect with the emotion of that moment in which you have complete and total happiness right in front of you on the big jumbo screen.

This saved image will be your anchor to the state of happiness. When you feel anxiety building, hit pause and recall this image anchor and just hold the image as you feel your energy shift from anxiety to happiness. Don't block this shift because, after all, this is how you should seek to feel all the time. This exercise will not only allow you to find and recognize that moment of happiness in your life, but will also give you a sense of gratitude for having so many moments of happiness to choose from.

We all long to live in perennial happiness, and the idea of doing so is not some myth or impossibility. Yes, your life will have difficulties, but having an anchor established that links you to a state of happiness will help you create a sense of calm and control. Your anchor is all you need to rediscover your goals, see clearly what you should do next, or determine if the path you are following is the right one.

This is a purely personal process. Each of us will find our image anchor and the emotion we wish to connect to that image. Other emotions you might want to create anchors for are feelings of safety and peace, or maybe confidence. Whatever you choose, I invite you to use the anchor image and emotion exercise whenever you feel it is necessary. The purpose is to be able to go back to your essence, to your moment of happiness, peace, strength, and your own identity so that you evaluate and replan or reinvent yourself.

Going back to Claudia's story one more time, it was necessary to take her to that energy state of being happy at the moment with this exercise. For her, that happy moment was when she connected with the people she was training. As she moved out of depression and into a more controlled, positive state of feeling, she returned to her essence, rediscovered her identity, and found her path forward. Once she had her horizon back in sight, it was necessary to create a plan to reach that horizon. To maintain momentum towards that goal, she had to repeat the anchoring exercise repeatedly to recognize that this was her greatest strength. Being back in control of her thinking and behaviors, she was able to find the solutions she needed to get back to doing what she loved and so closely identified with.

Each adversity that we face in life can become a positive experience. At first, we might not believe this because of how we feel at the moment. However, adversity will inevitably lead us to recognize our capabilities and strengths. And when we identify how to get out of the situation that creates anxiety, we find ourselves empowered through our resilience.

When you feel confused, sad, or have lost your identity or your way, look at your history. Then look at when you were happy and recreate that emotional state. Once you shift your emotional state, you will see a new path forward that will provide you with a new identity that includes the title resilient, amazing, adaptive woman.

"We cannot live only for ourselves.
Thousands of fibers connect us with our fellow human beings;
and in these fibers, like compassionate threads,
our actions generate causes and come back to us as effects."

Herman Melville

CHAPTER 4

SELF-ESTEEM AND SELF-WORTH

Self-Esteem and Self-Worth

Self-esteem is how we value and perceive ourselves. It's based on our opinions and beliefs about ourselves, which can sometimes feel really difficult to change. Your self-esteem can affect whether you like and value yourself as a person and can make decisions and assert yourself. Self-worth is the internal sense of being good enough and worthy of love and belonging from others. Self-worth is often confused with self-esteem, which relies on external factors such as successes and achievements to define worth and can often be inconsistent, leading to someone struggling with feeling worthy.

We can say that self-esteem and self-worth are related but different concepts of how we see ourselves and our value in the world. Self-esteem can be understood as a personal, subjective, individual view connected with our value system. It is emotional, and only we are responsible for its state. Because self-esteem is an internal perspective, it is necessary to always check-in on how we feel about ourselves. This checking-in and self-awareness leads us to a process called self-appraisal

In the mental health field, self-appraisal is the process of looking at oneself in order to assess aspects that are important to one's identity without placing judgment.

William James, American psychologist and philosopher, a graduate of Harvard University, and founder of functional psychology, introduced the psychological concept of self-esteem at the end of the 19th century in his work *The Principles of Psychology*. He had been studying the splitting of our "Global-Self" into the "Me" and the "I." According to James, from this splitting, we all become aware of the self and thus the self-esteem is born to a greater or lesser degree.

Now that I have set the foundation and made sure we were all using the same terms and understanding, I want to share with you the "Self-Esteem Ladder" presented by Rosenberg. The Self-Esteem ladder is one of the most widely used techniques to help clients evaluate self-esteem. The Self-Esteem ladder was initially developed in 1965. The scale includes questions that assess feelings of self-respect and self-acceptance, based on these precepts:

1. **Self-awareness:** implies recognizing oneself. Recognizing our needs, abilities, potential, weaknesses, bodily or psychological qualities, our actions. To be fully aware of who we are and where we are.

2. **Self-acceptance:** comprises accepting ourselves as we are, physically, psychologically, socially, and emotionally. Accepting ourselves and others by recognizing all the parts that make up who we are as a way of being and feeling.

3. **Self-assessment:** reflects the ability to evaluate and value the things that are good about oneself, those that satisfy us and are enriching, that make us feel good, that allow us to grow and learn. It comprises looking for and valuing everything that makes us feel proud of ourselves. It is about being able to praise our strengths over our weaknesses in any situation.

4. **Self-respect:** implies expressing and managing feelings and emotions in an active, controlled way, without hurting or blaming ourselves. Self-respect allows us to consider ourselves worthy of happiness, and it includes treating ourselves in the best possible way, without allowing others to mistreat

us. It is an absolute conviction that the desires and needs of each one of us have natural rights. And it is in being able to respect others with their individual rights, as well as to respect ourselves, that establishes our level of self-respect.

5. **Self-improvement:** If the person knows herself and is aware of her ability to change, and takes time to create a scale of values, develops and strengthens her capacities and potentialities. While accepting and respecting themselves, they will always be in a state of improvement. Self-improvement occurs when a person has a good level of self-esteem. Having a good self-esteem generates the ability to solve life's daily issues. Self-improvement is the sum of small daily achievements.

6. **Self-efficacy and self-dignity**. Self-esteem has two interconnected aspects:

   • A sense of winning or that sense of being able to get ahead (self-efficacy).

   • A sense of personal merit or worth (self-dignity).

   Self-efficacy allows us to have confidence in the functioning of the mind; it is the ability to think about the processes by which we judge, choose, decide. It is confidence in the ability to understand the facts of reality that fall within the sphere of our interests and needs; knowledgeable confidence in ourselves.

   Self-dignity is the certainty of our value; it is an affirmative attitude towards our right to live and be happy. It is that I am allowed to feel what I feel.

The lack of any part of these six parts of the ladder has an enormous effect on our mental and emotional health. Each part of the ladder represents a part of the whole that makes up the essence of self-esteem. These aspects or steps lead to a truthful self-analysis according to the role we are playing. The self-analysis that we often seek to be able to not only qualify our lives but to improve our lives. Without this truthful self-analysis, we could not move from where we are to where we envision ourselves and our lives to go.

An unhealthy relationship, be it a working relationship, a romantic relationship, or a family relationship, can best be defined as one that is negatively affecting our self-esteem on some level of the Self-Esteem Ladder. Let me point out that we, as adult women, are the only ones who grant permission for an unhealthy relationship to continue. To prevent the development or continuation of an unhealthy relationship, we must be aware of the need for boundaries. Setting and maintaining boundaries is the role of each of us as healthy adults. Think of boundaries as the limits and rules you set for yourself within a relationship. When you have healthy boundaries, you feel comfortable saying "no" to others.

In my practice this is a large part of my role; to help women identify and establish healthy boundaries or limits of tolerance. Most people have a mix of different boundary levels, so understand that one size does not fit all and that you need to be clear on what the exceptions are before they become crossed. Always remember, you are in charge of those exceptions.

Emotional health is like physical health, it is something that should become part of our daily health habits. We must always be busy identifying our self-esteem levels, constantly asking ourselves what to improve, not in terms of others, but in ourselves. Then, every day, determining what we have control over to become the best version of who we want to become.

Permissions Vs. Rights

All women should work on what permissions and rights they are giving away. By permissions, I mean the right for others to judge or define us, and to what extend we let these judgments and definitions affect us.

Consider Eliana, a patient who told me that when she was with her boyfriend, he frequently made disparaging remarks and insults. His remarks led her to cry and develop negative feelings of sadness and helplessness for several days following such encounters.

For this reason, one of the first things that I work on with my patients is to help them understand no one has the right to make us cry, feel small or disrespect ourselves and steal a day of happiness. No one has the right to dull the light that is within us.

I want to walk you through one exercise I recommend to aid my clients in performing a daily self-diagnosis. The aim is to be constantly evaluating yourself and checking in to make sure you are doing the right things to maintain your sense of a positive self-image and the boundaries required to do so. This exercise is for you, about you, and what you discover is just for you, so that you can decide what to do next. This self-evaluation will give you the feedback you need to know if it is necessary to redirect yourself and help you recognize your strengths over your weaknesses.

This is an internal and individual process that will allow you to strengthen yourself emotionally. I emphasize the fact that this is about you and you doing the work, because when you allow others to direct your emotions, you are giving them the power. Mental and emotional health is about you maintaining your personal power. You are the owner and controller of your emotions. If there is a situation affecting you emotionally or mentally, it is because you left a door open. It is you who has given the permission to affect you. I know this sounds harsh, but the simple fact is that as adults we choose who we let into our lives and how we allow them to behave. Taking back that control can be difficult, but it is possible, and you do not have to do it alone.

In today's world of full exposure and full disclosure on social media, it is easy to receive an endless number of comments and judgments. However, everyone is the owner of their actions and thoughts regarding these attacks. You are the one who decides how much the opinions of others can affect you and how much you share with others. It is in exercising control, setting boundaries, where the solid foundation of your self-esteem will be established.

If you allow others to affect you repeatedly by permitting them to enter your emotional space, then you are the one who must figure out why that door is open and make the necessary changes to reestablish those boundaries

As much as we would like to, we cannot change another person's thoughts or emotions. However, you can decide what you will do with their judgments and comments. For example, you get ready to go out, get dressed, apply your makeup, look in the mirror and like the way you look, but when you walk downstairs, someone makes a negative comment about the way you look. In that moment of criticism, you are the one who decides how you will allow those comments to affect you. You can continue to feel confident and safe in being able to say *thank you I am fine with how I look*, or allow what they said to control your emotional state and send you back upstairs in tears to change? Remember alone in the bedroom as you checked yourself in the mirror, you loved your look and were proud of the person you saw in the mirror. Your self-esteem was a ten out of ten. Now, with one comment, you have been thrown into a position of self-awareness and self-judgment. Standing there at the foot of the stairs, you have to be able to take a moment to recognize them as outside your situation and evaluate the comments.

In that moment you need to decide if you will allow what was said to affect you. You get to decide if you will continue to love your look and yourself, or if you will allow the judgment of others to control your self-esteem. Boundaries have been crossed. What will you do? Let me point out that there is a difference between feedback or advice and criticism. Feedback and advice is based on the questions you ask. Criticism is just someone's opinion given without solicitation.

"Thinking and Feeling," vs. "Saying and Doing."

As I have been telling you, when faced with everyday life situations, within our internal conversations, it is necessary to evaluate: are your thoughts driven by reason or emotion? Are they rational or emotional? Most times, the use of reason should prevail over the heart. The best first step starts by acting from conscious reality.

In the process of closing cycles, it is essential to make use of the processes of self-evaluation and self-assessment that we have discussed so you are not permanently susceptible to the repeating patterns of changes you are experiencing. If you remain in a state of constant self-evaluation, nothing will take you by surprise because you will be a work in progress and continually balancing and adjusting your emotions and actions in accordance with the objectives you intend to achieve.

Women are emotional by nature and design with a great capacity to think and reason. As the best of emotional and intellectual design, we must know our immense power to protect ourselves.

The process of closing cycles is essential, and I recommend that before being assisted by a professional, psychologist, or coach, you take a deep personal analysis and do good internal work. If you find it difficult to do it alone, then a trained professional will be necessary. From my experience, working with a trained professional will produce results faster.

Maria is a 54-year-old woman who suffered a traffic accident. In the accident, her face became quite disfigured and she had to undergo several reconstructive facial surgeries. Faced with this unexpected and unfortunate event, her life took a 180-degree turn. Between the accident and repeated surgeries, her self-esteem was very vulnerable. Her new internal belief of her beauty was based on invisible physical scars on her face. Long after she had healed and looked 'normal', when she looked in the mirror all she could see were the scars and disfigurement.

Maria was not a simple case to work with. There was a lot of internal healing and reconstruction required. Watching Maria recover her self-esteem was very satisfying. As a woman of vast experiences and successes, Maria needed to tap into that strength and find a new sense of identity and value beyond her looks. A part of that healing was helping Maria use the anchoring technique I shared with you earlier in this book. I needed to help Maria reclaim the moments that held great happiness. By bringing her back into that moment of happiness, she could heal from the inside out. She was doing deep self-exploration and continued examining everything positive in her life. She was able to feel more confident and reclaim a higher level of self-esteem. Maria will always have some visible sign of the accident; how she processes that reminder will always depend on her self-esteem and by continuing to do the hard work.

Maria experienced a type of grief caused by her complications from the accident. Being able to acknowledge that loss and accept what she could and could not control, it was possible for her to improve her self-esteem through anchoring. Anchoring gave her the time to do the deep work of acceptance and reconciliation to become the new woman that she sees in the mirror. Now she is able to look into the mirror without anger and frustration from that "why me" perspective that hunted her in the past. The deprogramming and reprogramming of her concept of beauty required a lot of work, but Maria did the work and is better now than ever before as a result.

By sharing Maria's story, I'm showing you that you are not only what you see in the mirror. You are more than the image in the mirror. There are the countless experiences, successes, virtues, and value of your lifetime. You are a unique and unrepeatable being, and only you can give yourself your true value.

I invite you to reflect on everything that Maria went through and how she could have felt, what she could have said or manifested in this situation. Above all, reflect on what she was able to achieve by being willing to find her self-esteem. I want to leave you with these questions so that you can incorporate them in any life situation where you feel your self-esteem processes are being disrupted. The questions are: What do I think about this situation? How should I evaluate this situation? How does this situation make me feel? How do I verbalize my plans to get out of this situation? The most critical question is: What have I decided to do? The only power you have is to *decide* what you allow to affect you, how far you will allow it to affect you, and then *do* everything you can to get out of this situation.

Time to Forgive Yourself

When I talk about setting time aside to do a self-evaluation, I want to stress this must be a conscious and constant practice that is done without judgment. The goal is not to shame yourself but to take an inventory of how you are feeling about yourself, your boundaries, and your mental and emotional health. This is an invitation to review what makes you feel bad, not from guilt or regret, but from what you need to rebalance or possibly establish boundaries for. I want to always stress the importance of treating yourself with love and affection. You can't make the changes you want from a position of shame and guilt. If something went wrong or did not turn out the way you had expected, you must be able to forgive yourself and move on.

However, forgiving yourself requires more than just putting the past behind you and moving on. It is about accepting what has happened and showing compassion to yourself. Facing what you have done or what has happened is the first step toward self-forgiveness. Forgiving yourself means to recognize yourself within the process of self-acceptance with the understanding that you can no longer change what happened; you can only change your reaction. Forgiving yourself means leaving that burden behind, letting go of negative feelings, and starting to live in the here and now. Forgiveness is to love yourself and to put your feet firmly back on the path of who you are and where you want to go.

Remember that you are the person you should take care of the most. You need to make yourself the priority. You might have heard the quote by Rupi Kau, "How you love yourself is how you teach others to love you." Until you are able to love yourself and place yourself as the priority, no one else will.

Each day, we need to accept and love ourselves as we are in the moment. Take time to recognize your strengths and weaknesses and celebrate your journey. I know from personal experience you can achieve everything you desire. Be sure of who you are and where you want to go. Don't let any internal or external hesitations hinder you.

Learning to Love Yourself Again

After you establish forgiveness, it is time to see the new you in the mirror, shake hands and start walking forward. Now is the time to see yourself and rediscover what makes you happy, to ask yourself where do you want to go in your life, and who you want to join you along this journey?

Learning to love yourself again is a very similar exercise to the anchoring exercise. Loving yourself starts by evaluating those moments when you felt happy and empowered. Reflect on a time when you were in tune with your purpose and felt completely in flow.

Do you remember those courses you wanted to take and couldn't? Maybe there was a trip you always longed to take or those cooking classes you were passionate about and were unable to complete. After mourning the loss of that opportunity and accepting what happened, you have to make a new plan with the best of the objectives and commit to start over. By doing so, you start to rebuild self-love.

Aura struggled as an adolescent. At seventeen, she ran away from home. Within a very short time, she fell in love and gave birth to her first child, a daughter. A year later, she had a second child, a son. At twenty years of age, she had the responsibility of a home, two children, and a husband. Gone were the parties with friends, the freedom to live her life as she pleased. The next seventeen years were spent married and raising her children. Her life was consumed with managing the household.

One day, life with all its demands required to her to look for a job. For the first time in twenty years, she was outside the home and meeting other people and having new experiences. Over time, she fell so madly in love with a co-worker that she left her husband and her children. It was a bold move, to say the least, but she felt this new love would offer her a chance to rebuild her life. Shortly after remarrying, she had her third child, another daughter, and had once again dedicated herself entirely to her family and husband, but this time she was also working on obtaining a degree.

At fifty-seven, Aura lost her second-born child, her only son. He died under tragic circumstances. Losing her son was followed by a very intense mourning process. Two years following the death of her son, her mother died. Once again, Aura struggled with the grief of the loss of her mother and at the same time she faced a divorce.

Now sixty-two, Aura found her life totally off course. Each day was filled with mourning the loss of her son and her mother and the realization that she had lived her life taking care of other people first. She had devoted herself to her husband and children in a self-sacrificing way. There was never space for her to express herself and her desires. Now alone, she felt a vast emptiness. She had reached a point where she did not know what or for whom she should live.

Aura had to go through a process of mourning and deep acceptance of these new realities. She went through each of the stages of mourning and acceptance carefully as they related to each of the circumstances she experienced: the death of her son, the death of her mother, the husband who left, and the daughter who has grown up, moved away and had a family of their own. In this process, she had to face herself, and place herself and her needs first and foremost above other people.

Aura had reached a point in her life where she was required to evaluate herself and her choices. She needed to have her feet firmly planted on a path of her own choosing. The first step was in accepting herself as she was and validating her abilities.

As Aura regained her footing, she got a new job and was able to earn enough to support herself and even had time to rediscover her passion for swimming. Starting from scratch, Aura found a new community and had many new experiences. She realized that she could be herself and place herself first and not feel guilty about it. She discovered a world beyond what she used to know and a new level of happiness.

All that Aura went through was difficult and there were moments of great joy mixed with moments of great sorrow, but Aura anchored herself in circumstances of happiness and held on to the dreams she wanted to achieve amid the process of emotional recovery. Most important was her self-esteem continued to increase more and more every day.

With her new sense of self-determination, she realized that her current story will not be her last. She is clear and confident that the next goal and the path she decides is her decision alone.

Aura's story is not unique, there are many other stories with more or less intensity but all with favorable and encouraging results, because she, like the other women I have worked with, was born with the capability to fight for what she wanted and deserved in life. Having a clear goal and a firm conviction and passion is the secret to moving forward and claiming the life you want. At sixty-two, Aura had to forgive herself, find herself, and love herself again.

Aura and countless other women have been able to move past the experiences and circumstances in their past and stand up, look at themselves in the mirror and find their worth. I know you can, too.

You are worthy of taking time to love yourself and find your future.

"The two most powerful warriors are patience and time."

Leo Tolstoy

CHAPTER 5

CREATING A PLAN

The Value of Time

I want to share with you a beautiful parable that I read some time ago. From what I can tell, it has no known author.

> *Once upon a time, there was an island on which all the feelings and values of man lived. Side by side, the feelings of Good Humor, Sadness, Wisdom, Greed, Pride, even Love lived. One day, it was announced to the feelings that the island was about to sink. Together, the feelings prepared their boats and set sail to find a new home.*
>
> *Somehow, in all the confusion and hurry, Love waited until the last moment to prepare. Just as the island was about to sink, Love asked for help. As Greed passed by in a luxurious boat, Love shouted out. "Greed, can you take me with you?"*
>
> *To which Greed responded, "I can't because I'm carrying too much gold and silver and there's no room for you."*
>
> *Love then asked Pride, who had a magnificent boat for help. And Pride carefully answered "I can't take you, Love. Everything is perfect here. You could ruin my boat." As the island began to sink, Love became desperate and turned to Sadness for help. Sadness did not even bother to answer, for she was so sad that she wanted to be alone and did not know how to answer to Love. When Good Humor passed*

in front of Love, standing on the shore, Love thought Good Humor will surely welcome be aboard, but Good Humor was so busy having a good time that she did not hear Love's call above the music and merriment on board and sailed on.

Suddenly Love heard someone calling. "Love, I will take you."

It was an old man who had called him. Love was so happy to be off the island that he forgot to ask the old man his name. Days later, when they reached the new island, the old man got off and left. Love realized how much he owed the old man. Love asked Wisdom, who was the old man that had helped him.

"It was Time."

"Time? And why is it that Time was the only one that helped me?"

And Wisdom, being full of wisdom, answered, "Because only Time can understand how important Love is in life."

The most important love you can have in life is the love you have for yourself. The gift of wisdom is the understanding that there is no more valuable gift we can give ourselves than the time to cultivate self-love.

We measure our life in increments of time. This makes time our most valuable asset. Therefore, we must use it wisely. Like me, I am sure you have, at one time or another, taken time for granted. When we are young, the value of time seems almost meaningless. We live life as it comes to us, without thinking about how we are trading time.

As we grow older or maybe just wiser, we see the limits of time and how time seems too short and too fleeting to accomplish all we desire. Phrases like, "maybe later" or "someday I'll have more time" become all too common in our vocabulary. If we are to live up to our full potential, we need to find a way of maximizing time.

That is why it is critical for us to not only set goals, but to chart a course to achieve them. The thing is, when we are able to see a plan in action and then watch those actions create the results we desire in the time we desire, it becomes a cyclical process.

When we begin to set action plans in motion, we achieve more success and fulfillment. Positive results lead to positive actions that then create the desire for more positive actions. Soon, everything that is related to planning and the fulfillment of our goals gives us a sense of wellbeing and fulfillment, and also, a sense of control over our lives and our time.

From the time you wake up, you are thinking about what you will do with the day ahead. Thoughts about what meals you will prepare, what is needed to be done around the home or office, your spouse, how you will help the children with homework; a thousand thoughts fill our mind and we try to piece them together inside the time we have each day. I think it is an almost intrinsic nature for us as women to measure time in terms of the acts we will do for others.

Unfortunately, in life there is no formal process to teach us how to plan for all that we must undertake. We seem to stumble forward in life, adding more and more tasks to our list without adding more hours to the day. As a result, we slowly let go of the things that matter most to us and replace them with the things that matter most to others, telling ourselves that "someday, when I have more time…" only we never regain that time.

It is important to know as parents that we are always teaching by example. When we stop talking about our goals and how we will achieve them, our children learn by observation that time cannot be managed and instead personal goals and dreams must be forfeited. If we want to teach our children the value of dreaming and having goals, we have to practice master planning from a practical point in our own lives.

As a high-performance, competitive athlete everything I do is part of a bigger plan or strategy. From the time I wake up, I have to calculate the hours and laps of training, how I will manage my clients and other duties at the office alongside my eating and social activates, to down time to recovery. In the planning, I develop consistency and the commitment to solitary training and determination to win the daily fight against time. To reach the goal that I have set requires not only physical strength but mental strength. Time is something I race against on and off the Ironman Course. Everything has to be planned for me to succeed. For some, this idea of everything being planned may seem restrictive or even dull. But for me, it is very freeing and empowering. Because I don't have time to get distracted by the things that don't matter, I am focused on the things that matter most and bring me the highest satisfaction in life. I also know that when a new opportunity or interest comes into my life, I have the discipline to fully enjoy it, free of distractions and guilt. Knowing what is important, having a plan to achieve it, and knowing I can follow through on that plan is a very freeing experience.

Now that you clearly understand the importance of the planning process, you might be asking: how do I put planning into practice?

First, let me point out that much of our learning and baggage on this subject of planning comes from our cellular memory, as we have already discussed. So, it is important to look at the achievements of our grandparents, our parents, our ancestors. Many of them have done what looked impossible, the unimaginable, to achieve their goals. For those that crossed oceans, fought wars, thrived in economic depression and political unrest, giving up was never considered an option. They have shown us with their journey that passion and planning were part of their success.

The elements of planning can be as simple or as complex as you would like them to be. The key is to not get lost in the planning and fail to execute. For now, I share with you a few thoughts that you must take into consideration when planning:

Diagnosis: If you have been actively taking part in the lessons I have shared with you, at this point you are clear about what you have gone through. You have accepted and validated the experience and you already have a full awareness of the here and now.

It is then time to ask yourself; "What do I have and what do I want to happen next?" When you take your car into the shop and the mechanic tells you: "Look, after checking it, the engine and the gearbox are bad; the radiator and the axles are good, but if you do not fix what I have indicated, it will not run." The mechanic has just offered you a diagnosis. Going over everything that needs to be fixed. It is the cost compared to the value that determines where you want to go next. The mechanic has made a diagnosis. A diagnosis on its own does not tell you the value of the car or how long it will continue to run. The diagnosis simply offers a review of the current condition without relationship to the cause. The diagnosis just makes it clear the strengths and weaknesses of the car.

Objectives: The objective or the target is about what you want. In the example of the car repair, the objective of getting the repairs might be that after the repairs, you want the car to last another twenty thousand miles. To answer if the objective is achievable, it is important to set yourself a micro-vision that is part of the bigger vision of where you want to get to. The micro vision is part of the ultimate goal, that final objective, that you aspire to reach, but on a smaller scale. Maybe it is about how to manage the next day or even an hour of your time in order to get to the larger objective. For me, being able to maximize my work time helps me know I am going to be able to achieve professional goals that help fund my competitive athletic goals. One micro goal can support another goal. Each micro goal is important on its own and also as support for the larger, longer vision. In short, it's casting your eyes and looking at the top of the mountain and knowing that it will take a series of carefully chosen steps to get there. Remember that success with any goal starts in micro-processes or the "baby steps."

Strategies: Taking the first step is great. Taking the first best step is a path to success. You must design your strategy to take those steps. It is in the details that we achieve more: more time, more momentum, more success. The difference between fifth and sixth gear on a bike may seem insignificant, but over the 112-mile Ironman course it can make a big difference. Strategy is choosing between any action and an intentional action. To build strategy, ask yourself the *how* of what you will do and not just the *what* you will do. You must think of what the most suitable and creative way is to take those small steps that will not leave you strained and stuck halfway to your goal. The *how* is also about knowing what will keep you motivated. Not every strategy you will follow will be completely in alignment with your personality or your current capabilities. My coach often reminds me to "run my race" which is really a strategy to ignore the desire for comparisons with other people. My job is to run the race I have planned based on my objectives and not worry whether another runner is faster or slower, if they are smiling or are serious. None of what is going on around me should matter. I need to trust myself, and my strategy is *my strategy*.

Resources: What are the resources you have at hand to achieve what you want? (And remember, time is a nonrenewable resource.) Resources include external tangible, such as economic, infrastructure, or intangible internal resources such as patience, perseverance, resistance to failure, adaptability, and flexibility. And there are human resources such as family, friends, teachers, colleagues, co-workers. Depending on your objectives, you will need to evaluate which resources will allow you to be more efficient and effective.

Time: Although time may seem an obvious part of your planning, it is necessary to establish timelines as part of your plan. As I already said, it is necessary to take advantage of every minute possible, and unless we structure within a timetable, it will never happen. Just like we have short, medium, and long-term strategies, we will need to develop short, medium, and long-term timelines for the actions we will take depending on the objectives. This will allow us to set concrete terms for the goal we want to achieve and when we will achieve them. In marathon racing, we talk about these as our mile splits. A split is a running and racing term that means the time that it takes to complete a specific distance. For example, if you're running five miles, your time at each mile marker is called a "mile split" Depending on the length of the race, you may have one-mile splits or five-mile splits or half marathon splits.

Runners use splits to see if they're pacing evenly and staying on track to hit a specific goal. The goal is to run your race based on your plan and your objectives and on your timeline, not based on the pace of runners besides you.

Evaluation: Evaluation is the constant process of review and reflection on how you are doing, what you are missing, what resources you may have to incorporate to make sure the strategy was effective to achieve the plan. Evaluation is also cyclical in that you must be disciplined when evaluating and understand that it is not a one-and-done process. Each change or adjustment in the strategy results in a new outcome that must be evaluated against the plan and the objective. The more open you are to the process of evaluation, the more likely you are to minimize the mistakes that can be made. Evaluation also gives you the possibility of correcting the course in a timely manner.

Action plan: None of what we have talked about will be of value if you don't write down your action plan. By being written, the action plan will allow you to be more concrete about what your objectives are, your timeline and your strategy and allow you to visualize the big picture. How and where you write it down is less important than being sure to write it. Give yourself permission to be creative, of seeing your action plan for yourself. Let the simple act of seeing it be one more motivation to move forward. It is a gift you give yourself. Let it be your best gift. The only requirement is that you must set a start date and a completion date.

Visualization: You can visualize your plain in a lot of ways. First, by forming a mental picture. You can use the anchoring technique that we have already discussed and anchoring that image of success to a word or feeling. You can also do it physically by creating a vision board using poster board. For example, if your goal is to graduate from a degree program, place a picture of yourself smiling and happy with cap and gown and maybe the logo of the university where you will graduate. If it is a new job you are seeking, look for the logo of the company, or cut out a picture of your possible office. Visualize where you are going, not where you currently are. You become what you create and what you believe.

Creating a vision of what you want to become will allow you to be focused on how you see yourself and connect with that emotion of joy, happiness and pride each time you look at that image.

Besides these elements that I have presented, you must also consider the following:

- The level of constancy will have a direct effect on your level of success. Remember that every new habit takes approximately twenty-one (21) days to settle in. Set a time and place to carry out your planning process, allow yourself the time to adapt and change and be aware that it is a day-by-day process.

- Planning is an act of love. First, it is an act of love to yourself to the extent that you plan a life for yourself. It is the extent to which you love and value yourself.

- Do not see it as a job. On the contrary, planning should be a moment of connection with the yearning, with the illusion of what you want to achieve, but also with reality, to contact with the here and now according to your objectives.

- When you start to plan, values must always be at the center. Values such as patience, constancy, tolerance, acceptance; all those that connect you with your chosen course.

- Establish a motivational anchor. It can be with a person, a place, an image, a smell, or any aspect that will bring you back on track when you feel you have lost your way. You will encounter obstacles along the way. It has happened to me; it happens to all of us, but you have to keep moving forward. You are strong and empowered, and having a motivational anchor will help you. Some people, in those moments of feeling defeated, look to social media for stories about those who have achieved a similar accomplishment and how they did it. Your story may be similar to others, but your journey is your own. Learn what you can from others, but trust yourself to know what is best for you.

- Everything in life is a learning process. In every experience, in every moment, there is always something to learn. Whether an experience feels pleasant or unpleasant, there is always something to learn. So, in that moment of evaluation, sit down for a while, outside of the experience, get away from what you may be feeling, and ask yourself, what should I learn from this experience? Never approach this moment from the perspective of victim, sadness, or despair. Ask yourself how can this experience strengthen me?

- You must also be flexible because planning has an element of emotions, circumstances, and other people as a part of it. Unfortunately, as much as we would like, nothing is linear. There are always unforeseen events in everything. Sometimes it is necessary to modify the original plan to achieve the desired results. Frustration will occur if you don't plan on being flexible.

- I can't stress enough that you must make your plan rather than allow someone else to make it for you. If you don't take charge of the plan, you will always be a part of someone else's plans. And when you are a part of someone else's plan, you will become a resource in someone else's strategies for success. And in doing so, you run the risk of living someone else's life and not your own. The idea is to be in complete control of your life and your plan.

- In the process of designing your objective you become laser focused on you and your objectives. Laser focus without distraction can be hard. To develop laser focus, you have to recognize the elements that can be potential distractions and develop a plan to minimize those distractions. Those distractions can be people, situations, circumstances, feelings and negative thoughts. The goal is to keep your eyes set on the goal with a sense of security and firmness. You are in control. See yourself like a racehorse with a pair of blinders. With those blinders, they cannot see the things on each side, so they can remain focused on the finish line.

- With planning, we can only plan for the present and the future. The past can only be left in the past. That is why it is important to reflect at the moment on what requires our attention here and now. It may sound cliché, but you cannot go back in time, nor live in the past. You can only look forward and only create a plan for the future.

- There are no magic formulas for creating a plan. There is no specific pattern, and each experience is unique, just like each person. Remember that you and only you are the owner of your plan. You know where you want to go, do not allow yourself to self-sabotage, or permit external intrusions to break your focus.

- You are the DESIGNER of your destiny. Planning will allow you to develop creativity in every sense of the word. Even in the most "insignificant" situations, you will have the ability to recalculate and replan in order to be highly efficient and effective.

An excellent motivational strategy that you can use is to make affirmations and mantras. Those little phrases that will program your brain for success can be a secret weapon to staying on your plan. Take these affirmation statements and place them strategically in all the possible places you will see them. Place them on your computer, on the fridge, next to the bed, on your car dashboard, even on the bathroom mirror.

I can tell you that at sixty-two years old, I looked at my life, and I am grateful for every planned moment. The sweet and bitter moments, the ups and downs, the joys and sorrows, every moment has been magical, and all have led me to be who I am today and for that I am grateful. Over the years, I have planned and replanned my career, my personal relationships, my studies, my sports. I have learned to accept the unexpected and I am confident that along the way the plans that I have made for me and by me have been the best plans. I want you to live your life with confidence that the plans you make for your life will always lead to your happiness and a sense of worth. I want to tell you that you are valuable simply because you are a woman and that you have the power to make and carry out powerful life transformational plans.

Adapting to Changing Time

Understand that the meaning of the word adaptation is modification, accommodation, or adjustment to a place, a situation, or people different from the usual ones, which implies an emotional and cognitive shift.

Since we are unique beings, each adaptation has many variables, and nothing is linear or objective. On the contrary, the subjectivity of emotionality reigns. Therefore, we must adapt ourselves to this new era of globalization, technology, social networks, climate change, and pandemics. It is necessary to accept that there is no other way, no other planet, no other reality. We cannot wrap ourselves up or put ourselves in a glass capsule and simply wait in hiding. It is time to adapt to this new scenario.

When you make planning part of your daily work, you diagnose the circumstances, evaluate your tools and undertake an action plan that adapts to an ever changing environment and reality.

I would like to share Carolina's story of how she had to both plan and adapt. Carolina is a 38-year-old professional teacher who, because of the pandemic, decided to adapt her profession to the tool she was using the most, social networks and the internet. To continue with her plan in a changing environment, she made videos, all very creative, although not from a formal plan of what she wanted to do or where she wanted to go. Using social networks and video led to her accelerating her success as a teacher and allowed her to establish economic independence for the first time. This sense of independence gave her a feeling of empowerment and motivated her to continue to adapt and grow in the new circumstance.

At the same time, she met a young man, who at first supported and encouraged her. As time went by, he realized he had a successful and determined woman by his side, and feeling threatened, he began to find ways to erode her self-esteem, hoping to diminish her independence. Carolina, lacking a clear plan for her business, began to doubt herself and her success. Little by little, she began to lose the students she had. She stopped having the necessary consistency to keep the business growing, let alone stay afloat. So, she lost more and more students. She was slipping backwards both personally and economically. She remained in the toxic relationship along with all the hardships and the negative emotions. She gained weight, and she no longer had the sense of independence or confidence she had just a few months earlier. Several situations led her to seek my support as a specialist, psychologist, and Life Coach.

To help her begin to recover what she had lost required specific sessions and techniques to rescue her self-esteem, self-worth, and self-love. Once that recovery was underway, she needed to regain the understanding of the value of her skills and abilities and to apply powerful anchors to those moments when she was most empowered and successful. Having these anchors would help her establish a plan for becoming stronger and healthier emotionally, professionally, economically. Carolina was the first to acknowledge that she had let herself go and accepted each of the steps she would have to take to fulfill her plan. Little by little, she restored the necessary facets of her life. But one of the most complex issues was for her to determine if she needed to end the abusive relationship.

She has managed to restore her business, and she has had such a positive response from the beneficiaries of her training proposal that she is considering hiring colleagues to help manage the growing student enrollment. Her new path is now built with a firm, clear and focused plan and strategy.

Carolina story is an example of how important it is to plan every aspect of our life. When she stopped living her plan and started living by and for others, she lost focus of her talents and her worth. Carolina had all the tools for success. She just lost sight of them for a time. I know what you're thinking, "who you fall in love with can't be planned". The truth is the who, maybe not, but the what can be. Had she built into her plan that the person she would love would be someone that spoke words of encouragement to her, that supported her independence and business sense she might have not lost focus because of a relationship. Instead, she would have gained a resource that helped her achieve her plans. So yes, plan even who you will fall in love with. You're worth the best kind of love. The type of love that celebrates you and your plans.

Where you are is where you are and unfortunately, there are no do-overs, no way to go back to the past. The good news is there is a new future waiting for you. With the lessons you have learned, acquired through hardship, like Carolina, you are much stronger. What you have, your daily life, has come about from the habit of planning or maybe lack of planning you did in the past. By following the outline for building a plan shared with you in this chapter, you will realize the rewarding feeling that you get when you reach a goal. Those things that used to seem impossible become your reality. You know you can do it. If you look closely at your past, you will see that you did it once before. You can do it again and again. All that you need to do is build a plan, set a strategy, use time to your advantage and never lose focus on your worth. Make these tools your best allies to fulfill and achieve those goals. The road to success awaits you. Plan it, live it, and enjoy it!

"He who has a way to live can face all the 'hows'."

Friedrich Nietzsche

CHAPTER 6

BACK TO THE MAP

Maps Matter

Within the previous chapters I have shared many lessons and have asked you to do some serious self-examination and work in each of those chapters Now that you have done the work of the previous lessons and understand better what I am trying to share with you and why it is so important to recognize and validate your feelings and accept yourself according to your emotions, you are ready to get back on the map with all the awareness of your strengths and weaknesses. You are ready to put into practice a plan that allows you to recover your truth and move boldly into your full life.

Has this ever happened to you on a drive? You start out knowing the course you will take, the time it will take and even the roads to avoid and then suddenly you get disoriented and feel lost? What you thought was a two way road became a one way and what you thought would only take a few minutes quickly turned into an hour detour. I know I am not the only person who has experienced this. So, what do you do when that happens? Simple, pull over to the side and pull out the map. Take the time to study it and figure out where you really are versus where you want to be. Look around for reference points; if you need to, phone a friend and ask for help. Don't take the next step until you manage to find your bearings and are confident about getting back on your route.

No matter how long or short a trip you take, there is always a bit of preparation in advance. Looking for the suitcase, packing and thinking about what you may need. Without fail, you will get this feeling that you are missing something, making you stop and analyze what you have and what you do not have. The great thing about new adventures if it's to an unfamiliar place, you can often hire a guide, an expert who will take you under their wing and make sure you get the best experience possible. The journey that you are about to embark on is one you have prepared well for, and you have not only your vision as a guide, but so many others waiting along the journey to help you.

For now, let me be your first guide and together we will go through this chapter and prepare your map for the journey ahead. The journey ahead may seem overwhelming, but relax, I am there with you. I know the emotions you are feeling may have left you a little disoriented. That is normal. I know you must also have a lot of questions; what do I do now, where do I go, how do I get there, who can help me? That is normal too. That is why I am here. I will be your guide. You can count on me. I have been where you are and have helped hundreds of women move past the fear and into their dreams. We will go at your pace and we will achieve what I have promised!

The first step on our journey is what I call creating an Emotional Reorientation. Emotional Reorientation is realigning your emotions to the vision or dream you have for your life. When you re-orientate a map, sometimes you adjust the map and sometimes you adjust yourself to the map. Neither is right nor wrong. The goal is to create alignment with where you are to where you want to go. For Emotional Reorientation, we adjust our emotions, so they are aligned as much as possible with the goal we want to reach. This Emotional Reorientation process is not a one-and-done process, because our emotions can cause us to lose our direction, we can easily get carried off track. Feelings of anger, sadness, frustration can be strong detractors, and it is at that moment that you must recognize the need to reorient your emotions. You have to be able to stop seeing the glass half empty and start seeing it as half full. Stop asking "why me," and instead ask: "what should I learn from this?"

Having an awareness of where you are regarding your emotional alignment or orientation will help you break old, learned habits and discover new skills that will allow you to be more objective. By being more objective you can separate your emotions from your circumstances.

The expectations and judgments (both internal and external) we face daily, along with the fear of not being enough, make up the unconscious patterns that limit us. These negative emotions make our belief system convert all that we have in our favor into limitations. That is why it is necessary and critical to be able to reorient ourselves emotionally and identify self-limiting, self-sabotaging thoughts and behaviors that for so long have been limiting our dreams and delaying our progress.

These limiting beliefs could have been planted in our unconscious during the formation of our identity. They could also be associated with an emotion that you can't identify the cause. Being out of emotional orientation is like being a beautiful woman the world values, but internally you see are yourself as the ugly duckling. This feeling of being less than the rest and unwanted takes hold in our thoughts and we feel powerless and paralyzed.

That misplanted belief can be so powerful that it often requires the guidance of a professional to uproot it. Someone who will delve into the person's mind to find the moment when the event became anchored with the corresponding emotion and became part of the person's belief system. Neurolinguistic programming puts it as learning to unlearn. That may sound like a strange contradiction, but it is the key to the emotional reorientation. Often, we are seeking something while not knowing what we are looking for. The actual goal is to learn how to leave behind all those learned thoughts that in one way or another make us feel insecure, fearful, incapable and create new healthy positive emotions. Eliminating any limiting belief or feeling that inhibits our freedom and growth involves courage, conviction, and perseverance.

To achieve that freedom and growth, we have to be clear that our past does not define us, and we have in our hands the power and the possibility of changing all those negative concepts.

About sixteen years ago, after I was established in the United States, I treated a young girl named Anaís. She was a pleasant and capable young lady, but I knew something was not right because her mother always accompanied her to the sessions. When I spoke privately with her mother, I was struck by her mother's recurring comments about her daughter. The mother would often suggest that her daughter would achieve nothing, that she was stupid, had no intelligence, and that although she recognized her daughter was nice and had a good figure, she saw nothing beyond that.

I never allowed the mother to verbalize any of this in front of her daughter, but it was clear that she was constantly implanting these negative thoughts and feelings in the young girl outside of my office. As I investigated the root of the situation, I discovered that this mother was the only daughter of five siblings; so as a young girl, she was assigned the housework, never allowed to study for a degree, and always stayed at home. And when the time came, she moved from her parents' home to her husband's home and carried on with her assigned role with the same functions. The young lady's mother never knew another reality, and had always felt minimized without personal fulfillment.

This woman's frustration and anger were constantly projected towards the daughter. From her mother's beliefs, values, and identity system, the young lady's emotional ordination was developed at both a conscious and unconscious level. Changing Anais emotional ordination and belief patterns took me years of work. However, once the cause was identified, I was able to begin a process of counseling that led her to graduate from college as a social worker and become a successful professional. Despite Anaís's achievements, the mother continued to discredit these accomplishments. She would state that she did not know how her daughter had gotten so far; it must have been a matter of luck. Today, I continue to guide Anaís's hand to help her develop new strategies to reinforce her strength and self-identity. After years of hard work, Anaís has learned to reorient herself and break out of old established patterns. Anaís's story is a clear case of how self-limiting patterns can be generated in a person.

With NLP, or neurolinguistic programming, the approach for changing the belief system is purely behavioral. NLP focuses on reason over emotion and to unlearn the anchors associated with negative emotions and beliefs. The goal is to learn to use the brain to feel good and to replace old emotions and beliefs. The key is to implant new ideas or patterns with new cognitive and emotional anchors.

Since each of us is a unique and unrepeatable being, it is necessary to evaluate which tool is most appropriate for you and your situation. What I want you to understand is that there are several processes and techniques used when you work with a professional to identify those emotions that need to be reoriented. And each of these processes requires patience, love, care, delicacy, and at times a steel fist in a silk glove, because emotions cannot be handled linearly or quickly. Emotions operate on several planes in several dimensions and require a constant back and forth to achieve the needed reorientation.

Building Your Personal Map

At this point, you recognize your strengths and weaknesses, and you know how to reorient this emotional process. What I want to offer you is a series of statements that will allow you to align yourself on your map. Equipped with these statements, you can create new routes whenever you feel it is necessary. Simply remember that this is a process of emotional reordination and is part of the daily work of recreating yourself and moving into alignment with your dreams.

Use any or all of the following statements and questions when you need to check your emotional orientation.

- Which of my identities is being affected right now (mother, daughter, wife, worker, student, relationships, friendships, etc.)?

- Which of my strengths can I call on that will help

me find myself again?

- Which of my weaknesses are being challenged right now? Can I manage this alone, or do I need support?

- What are the circumstances in which I constantly self-sabotage myself?

- What goal do I aspire to reach?

- How clearly am I visualizing the ideal situation?

- Next, take a moment and set a big goal.

- Outline small objectives that allow you to move step by step towards the ultimate goal.

- Make discipline and self-determination your best allies.

- Be patient and stay focused on the goal.

- Be open to identifying moments of weakness and reorient yourself emotionally.

- Look for allies who can help motivate you and help you reclaim your strengths.

- Stay away from negative people who seek to delay your growth.

- Appeal to all the fundamental elements to achieve your goals.

- Visualize yourself constantly living your dream. It will help you stay focused.

- Do activities that make you feel good: read, swim, study, dance, sports, gym. Take time for yourself.

Building You Relationship Map

At various times, you may encounter a variety of negative personal relationship changes, whether due to divorce, death, toxic relationships, or possessive friendships. In any situation involving feeling inadequate or connecting with negative emotions, you can feel stuck. When that happens, what should you do? Consider going back to this personal relationship map using the steps I outline below It is not necessary to perform these steps in any order, nor will it always be necessary to perform all of them. As I have shared with you, each person and situation is different and will require a bit of customizing. My goal as your first guide is to show you a reflective process that will allow you to identify the path you have taken, where you may have lost your north star, and how to get reorientated on your personal relationship map. What I am about to share is not a quick fix, but remember, you are what you create in your mind. Go ahead, create.

- Try to recognize the situation or person that anchors you with a particular negative emotion (fear, sadness, pain, helplessness, frustration, anger).

- Accept that you cannot change that past situation as it is part of the past. What has happened can't be undone. So, accept it and prepare to move forward.

- Pause and look at the here and now, identify what is possible to change.

- Visualize how you want your future to be, not from an energy of anxiety of uncertainty, but from a place of confidence.

- Recognize your limitations, and if it is necessary to seek help, do it! There are people who are trained for these issues and have the tools to guide you in this process.

- Know your strengths. No matter how small you think they may be, always keep them in mind. You will use them.

- Establish clear objectives and a clear time-frame. Time-frames are relevant because they will allow you to advance steadily, without hurry, and without pause.

- Act. Don't stop at just planning. Your actions must be concrete.

- Establish clear limits with yourself and with others. Be aware of the extent to which you allow the opinions of others to affect you or influence your emotions or decisions.

- Learn to say "NO" when necessary. This reinforces the previous action, but be clear that you will not do anything from a position of guilt but from your valuation.

- Be constant, persistent, and patient. Perhaps the road ahead will not be easy, nor as fast as you would like. But everything is part of a process. Live each moment because each one holds a lesson.

- Grow with the experience. The idea is to find yourself on a path to becoming stronger. Be aware of the road you travel and sure of the goals you want to achieve. Trust yourself.

As I said initially, none of this is a magic recipe or a quick fix because delving into your emotional issues and interpersonal relationships involves taking on many layers of discovery and change. It is essential to keep in mind that this is a process in which you and you alone decide to undertake and continue, often with the help of experts in the field.

Always remember that it is NOT in your hands to change another person's truth. The husband will not leave the lover and return. The abusive boyfriend will not be the one to change his ways. It will not be the jealous and possessive friend who, at some point, will change. Only YOU can change the situation and how it affects you. It is not a simple task, but needs to happen. You have the permission to fail from time to time but also the obligation to get up and keep trying because the only things that no one can steal from you are your dreams and the desire to achieve them.

Building Your Professional Map

In this area, the variables can also be diverse. Maybe you are not assigned high levels of responsibility in your job because you have created a silent message that you do not believe you are capable. You have convinced yourself that because of your age, education, skills, or experience that you are not worthy of the promotion or success you truly want. Maybe somewhere along the way you disconnected with the organizational mission or vision. As with the personal relationship map, writing the professional relationship map is a way to return alignment with your primary interests and professional purpose. You want to return to a sense of fulfillment in your profession so that you feel comfortable, valued, and motivated. To achieve that sense of purpose and professional alignment, here are a few questions to ask yourself to help you get back on track.

- Do I feel satisfied with what I am doing?

- Am I motivated?

- Are my ideals and values compatible with those of the organizational structure in which I find myself?

- What can I do to change this reality?

- Can I suggest areas for improvement for the organization that will help me reorientate?

- If I am not listened to, what decision should I make?

- Can I stay in this field, or can I venture into something that I am more passionate about?

- What should I do?

- When should I do it?

- Who can help me?

Asking yourself these questions can lead you to make several decisions, from proposing structural changes within the organization to which you belong or maybe even taking a different direction from the one you are in, either within the same industry or venturing into others. In either case, it implies that you will need to:

- Develop a professional preparation plan.

- Establish short, medium and long-term timelines.

- Set clear objectives and goals.

- Take advantage of your strengths and modify weaknesses.

- Work on potential areas for improvement.

- Update your skills to meet the current labor and technological needs.

I want to take a minute and address the current world situation. Until recently, many people were comfortable in their daily work routine, but then came the pandemic, and life was affected by so many unknown and unfamiliar circumstances. Many companies closed, and many reduced their staff. During all this, there are those that changed their industry or careers, as well as those that have created or have adapted to new technologies. In all of this, it became necessary to become slightly more competitive and get going. Lowering your arms and giving up is not an option.

To reinforce the previous point, let me share the story of Maria, who lives in South America. She trained as a secretary and started working as a young woman without a fixed goal in mind. Her training allowed her to gain a level of knowledge in the areas of writing, spelling, calligraphy, interpersonal relations, and several other things. After going through the training, she started a job with a nice schedule and a clear list of responsibilities. Something about what she was doing left her feeling uneasy. Although the pay was good, the monotony of her duties made her feel overwhelmed and unmotivated. As hard as she tried, she just did not connect with this work environment.

As she considered her options, she recognized her love of working with children, so she trained to become a professional teacher. At twenty-three, she graduated with honors as a teacher and was one of the first in her class to get a job offer. As a teacher she appreciated putting what she had studied to use and how her day was structured. Over the years, the pay diminished because of changes in her country's economy. Even at the university level, she reached a point that it was no longer enough to work in one job to make ends meet, that she had to take a second. Eighty percent of her time was devoted to her work in order to have some economic stability. Maria knew she was giving up a lot by working so much.

When the pandemic hit, all the schools closed. Somehow, in all that was happening, she reinvented herself. She quickly adapted to new technological tools as was required to keep teaching, but she was not happy, and the teaching situation was not what she wanted. Much to her regret, she made the radical decision to resign from each of her teaching jobs. She quit despite the advice of people around her who reminded her over and over of the job stability and the future retirement program. It was an emotionally hard decision. Soon after quitting, the negative feelings of nostalgia, sadness, and helplessness set in. Despite all her training, years of professional practical experience, and the recognition from her students, representatives, and colleagues, she let herself become depressed.

She found herself face to face with a reality that she had not wanted to accept for some time, and it was only because of the pandemic that she returned to her professional relationship map. When she did, it became clear that there was no way to choose what to do next. Moving forward was the only option. Thus, amid this whirlwind of emotions, she set up a space in her house, and through donations, she got the furniture to turn that space into a small classroom. During the pandemic, with all the required safety measures, she began to provide personalized teaching to some children in her community.

She looks back at that time as one with satisfaction. Her husband and children were also a great help in creating and growing her new business. When the time came for Maria to return to the classroom, she decided not to. After all, she now has her own tutoring business, earns an income that fits her needs, and she works from home. This new role allowed her to be an educator and still provide emotional support for her children. In other words, in this mass exit in the workplace, Marie was able to secure a new job with great benefits and a sense of independence. She could have had this life a long time ago, but it was only through adverse circumstances that she discovered a purpose and found a role that fulfills her both professionally and personally. She continues to educate herself and maintain the quality that has always characterized her, and now she has the time to venture into other areas as well. She also started to write a book. By needing clarity, Maria returned to her professional relationship map. As she did so she went through a carousel of emotions, fell down, recognized herself, and got up again, perhaps with many more strengths than when she started the journey.

Maria is an example of the reality that many are going through— feeling lost and the need to find themselves again. Like Maria, women are empowered, risk-takers, intelligent, and capable of facing any challenge. By realigning our personal and professional relationship maps and sticking firmly to them, each of us are able to gain the clarity and ordination we need to obtain our goals.

I want you to know that everything that happens to you in life is for a reason and a purpose. Therefore, you must always be alert, attentive, positive, and with true psychological and emotional depth, ready to detect and take advantage of opportunities that come your way.

I suggest you read this chapter whenever you feel a little confused and need to regain a sense of orientation in your life or career. Look inward and reorientate yourself with the woman you truly are. Know that you can do everything; you simply need to set out to do it. Your strength and courage are UNLIMITED. All the best!

I LOVE YOU SO MUCH!

CONCLUSION

This is a book to keep on your bedside table, always available in times you feel down or you have to live through what I call micro-hard times. I hope you will find within this book the processes to comfort you and guide you. I want you to know that I will be here, to be your guide on your journey.

I understand that every process is different, every situation is unique, but surely in that moment when you feel aimless, I invite you to recognize and accept your situation, your emotions. Always remember that everywhere there are stories similar to yours, perhaps with greater or lesser intensity. There are many brave women and fighters who are standing up to get ahead and refuse to let themselves fall. Use these stories as examples to follow. Always accept with wisdom and firmness your reality including what is not in your hands to change. That is one of the first steps of moving forward toward success.

Always remember during your journey to keep in mind the following premises: do not judge yourself, be patient, always keep an open mind to all possibilities. Let everything flow; trust and accept that everything will surely pass, and you will find the way forward.

Always keep in mind who you are and where you come from. Your identity will be the key to regain confidence, always considering your strengths and weaknesses. A strengthened self-esteem will allow you to value yourself and, to the extent that you can you love and value yourself, people around you will treat you the same way. You are YOUR greatest love. You are unique and incomparable. Always keep in mind the permissions and rights that you give yourself and those you give to others. Do not be afraid to say

NO, when necessary. The decisions or actions you make should be those that lead you to a greater path of happiness. Allow nothing or anyone to upset your esteem; do not leave that door open! And, if something should happen, review and redirect again towards the right path.

YOU ARE THE OWNER OF YOUR EMOTIONS AND DECISIONS. Keep this belief with you at all times.

To guide this new path and make decisions, a planning process is always necessary. Remember that a well-planned process will lead to sure success. Therefore, it is important to make a good diagnosis.

Be clear about what you have, in the here and now. Set objectives and goals you want to reach and the small steps that will take you there, with simple time lines. Be a great strategist. Always guide that path in an effective and efficient way. Always plan how you are going to get there. Having these processes in place will help you even in the unforeseen. Evaluate all the resources in your favor and even those that you must incorporate. One of the most important aspects of this planning process is time. Remember that the goals you set for yourself must be designed in a workable time and space frame. And not everything will be done at once. Some things will be done in the short-term and other will be long-term, but this aspect must be fundamental so that you don't get stuck.

A key tool is the action plan. It will always give you an overview for constant evaluation. What have you done, what are you missing, how are you doing, what to improve, remove or incorporate? Visualize yourself. Always go beyond. Don't forget that YOU ARE WHAT YOU CREATE AND WHAT YOU BELIEVE, because you alone are the DESIGNER of your destiny.

This entire process will allow you to recenter your map, renew yourself, get back on track and know that it is YOU who leads the way. Reorient yourself emotionally. Do not allow yourself to be sabotaged internally or externally. Each of these situations has a series of premises that will allow you to guide the way. Review them, read them, adapt them, improve them. The concept is that you know how and where to go to reconnect with that woman who was happy at some point and who needs to return to that wonderful place of self-respect and self-love. I will be here to guide your way. In these pages I will always be here as a friend, mentor and guide. You are not alone. Let's walk and always go forward. Remember:

YOU CAN! THAT'S FOR SURE!!!

A PART OF ME

I want to share with you something that is very important in my life, and that is the art of my father, Santiago Szriftgiser. He was a great surrealist artist. He was a student of Juan Battle Planas.

Among the many exhibitions that he presented, there is one that I must highlight, as it holds special pride for me. It is the mural at the entrance of the great San Martin Theater in Buenos Aires, Argentina.

The painting I chose for the cover of my book is one of the many in his collection titled *¡Toda una vida en el arte!* and I chose it precisely because it evokes a feeling of planes, dimensions, windows and figures that suggest the past, present and the future. I leave it open to what it suggests to you. As for each of us, beautiful women, I am happy that you are striving for more in your life. For more positive changes in your lives. For more personal achievements. That you are seeking greatness and expanding your horizons for mental and physical health, your sacred temple. I applaud you for taking this step to learn to take care of yourself and to love yourself more and become more focused on our life goals and personal desires.

My next book will inspire you to take care of yourself at the next level with a detailed plan of action, especially for women (who obviously have a different endocrine system than men), to train for a road race be it a 5K or a marathon. I will take you step-by-step and help you put one foot in front of the other.

I want to show you that we can start training at any age and that it's just a matter of setting your mind to the task and getting started. It's a simple fact that when you look good, you feel better!

I hope you have enjoyed this book. I put a lot of love into writing it, and I hope it will serve as a guide for you when you need it most.

I respect, admire and love you very much, woman!

ABOUT THE AUTHOR

With over forty years of professional experience in the mental health field, Patricia has had an outstanding and prolific career. She has a degree in Psychology from John F. Kennedy University in Buenos Aires, Argentina. She has postgraduate studies in psychoanalysis.

In the United States, she obtained her L.H.M.C. degree in Counseling (L.H.M.C.), in the State of New York.

In addition, she is a *life coach*, a multilingual psychotherapist who specializes in individual, adolescent and couples therapy, trained in international crisis management, sport psychology and post-traumatic stress disorder (PTSD).

IPatricia also holds BC-TMH (Board Certified Tele Mental Health) credentials, which allows her to offer therapy or life coaching sessions on an international level.

Patricia directed the Ground Zero mental health services team during the terrorist attack of 9/11/2001 by providing psychological assistance to the survivors and the victims.

She also served as mental health response team member to the Jewish community during the bombing in Buenos Aires, Argentina in 1994 (AMIA-1994). Patricia was a professional participant in the psychological assistance in trauma work in the bombing of the Israeli Embassy in 1992.

Patricia is an expert in PTSD assisting war veterans, survivors of terrorist attacks, survivors of sexual abuse, women survivors of human trafficking and domestic violence.

She has been featured in various media outlets, including 60 minutes, CNN, NBC, and has published several articles in the Wall

Street Journal and New York Times. She has also been a guest host on several international podcasts, live casts and radio show.

Philanthropy and service are pillars in Patricia's life. She is the founder and president of My Power Foundation, an NGO (501-C3), active for eleven years with many exemplary projects of global help.

He is also a board member of the Jewish Family Service and Children's Center of Greater Clifton-Passaic, New Jersey USA.

Patricia is an internationally recognized high-performance competitive athlete having taken part in, and won awards in, several Half Ironman (70.3-mile) courses and Full Ironman (140.6-mile) courses. Patricia qualified and won her group in Mar del Plata, Argentina 2019, and will compete in the Ironman World Championship in Kona Hawaii to be held in 2022.

She has completed twenty New York City Marathons and fifty-five marathons internationally to date.

Patricia is a professional skydiver, certified scuba diver, yachtsman (American Sailing Association), spinning instructor, mountaineer and has climbed the Lanin volcano in Patagonia, Argentina.

Patricia has a strong background in nutrition and supplements, which, coupled with her experience in sports psychology, is a perfect combination to assist individuals in achieving their personal goals at all levels, athletic and personal.

Everything she does is with the heart of a lion, the spirit of a warrior, and the understanding that she, like all women, can do everything she dreams.

www.ingramcontent.com/pod-product-compliance
Lightning Source LLC
Chambersburg PA
CBHW071020120626
46546CB00003B/1168